AMERICAN TOYSCAPE

A photobook brought to you by photographers from around the United States, the American Figure Circle!

FIGURE CIRCLE USA
PRESENTS

PREFACE

"Creativity is the way I share my soul with the world" – Brene Brown

What is the purpose of art if it is not shared? Indeed, our desire to share our creations drives us, inspires us, and allows us to develop communities and lifelong friendships.

Who are we? We are a group of photographers from the United States with a passion for collecting anime figurines. Fortunately, our passion expands beyond mere possession! Through taking pictures and sharing our works, we found a community with people of similar interests and have grown together to where we are now!

Inspired by other international groups such as Figure Photo Studio (FPS) and Nendonesia, we hoped to produce a photo book and social community that was equally as strong in the United States. Thus, the photo book project was born!

In May 2016, a photographer by the handle of Stereometric invited several figurine photographers around the United States to participate in the first American Figure Photobook project. As the project's name implies, the book's overall theme features the United States. Each photographer highlights special landmarks, activities, and/or themes from their respective region in the country whilst adding their unique style to the image.

Through this project, not only would we be able to showcase several talented photographers from the United States, but it would also highlight the diversity of our country and the artistic talents of the group – a melting pot of teamwork and passion for our work!

Although the project had great momentum, unforeseen circumstances caused the project to come to a grinding halt that inevitably led to a hiatus.

Two years later, on February 2018, four photographers from the previously invited collaborators came together to revitalize the project. This time, as the hobby had grown formidably since then, the group's determination solidified! We then invited several additional collaborators to participate in the photobook. After several months of planning, deliberation, design implementation, and test drives, we finally produced the product you now hold in your hands. This book exists as a physical manifestation of our passion, work, and love. Not only do we hope this will inspire you to perhaps consider an endeavor of your own, but to also give you a peek into how we seek to turn the ordinary into the extraordinary!

Without further ado, we humbly present:

The American Toyscape!

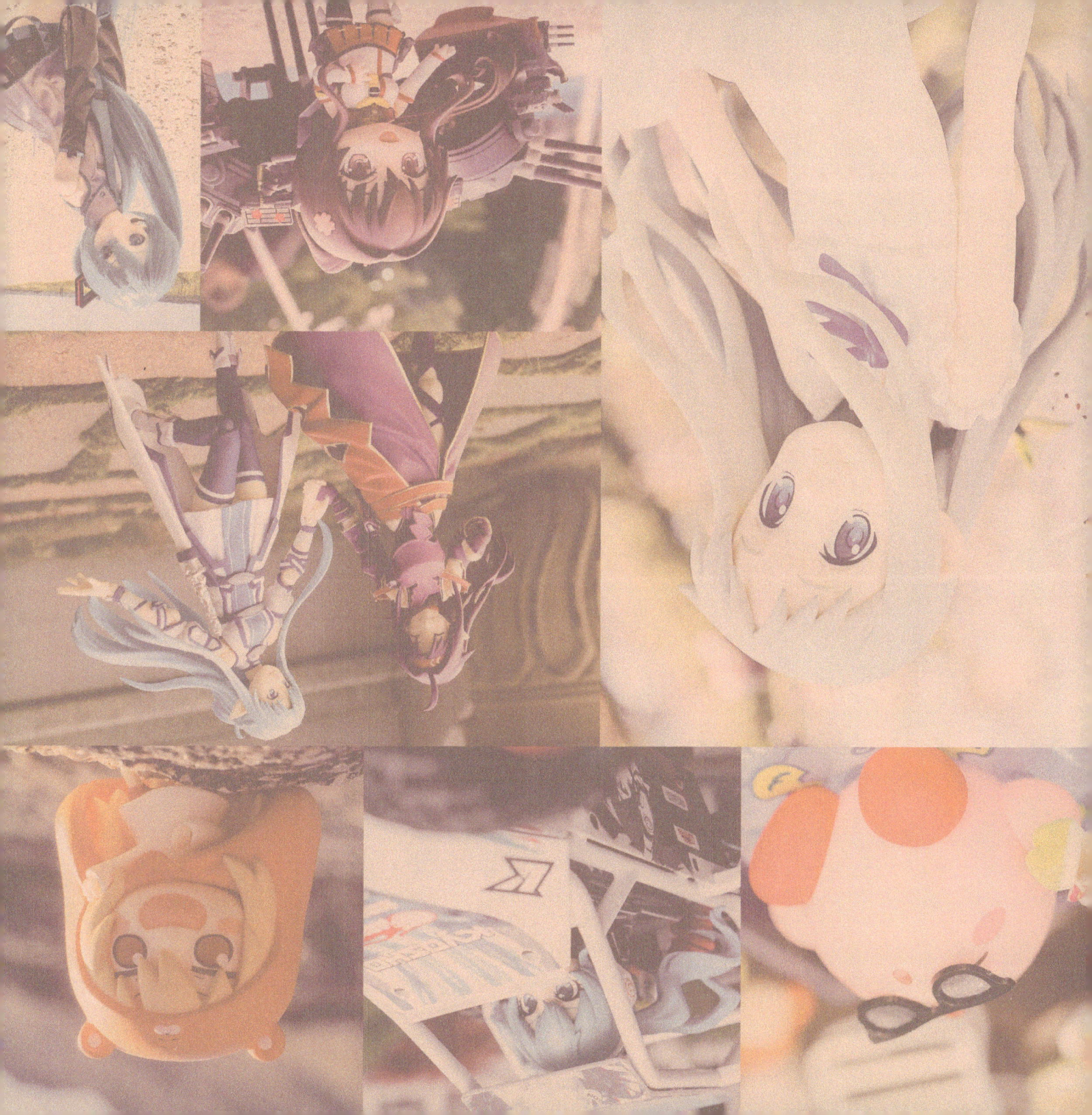

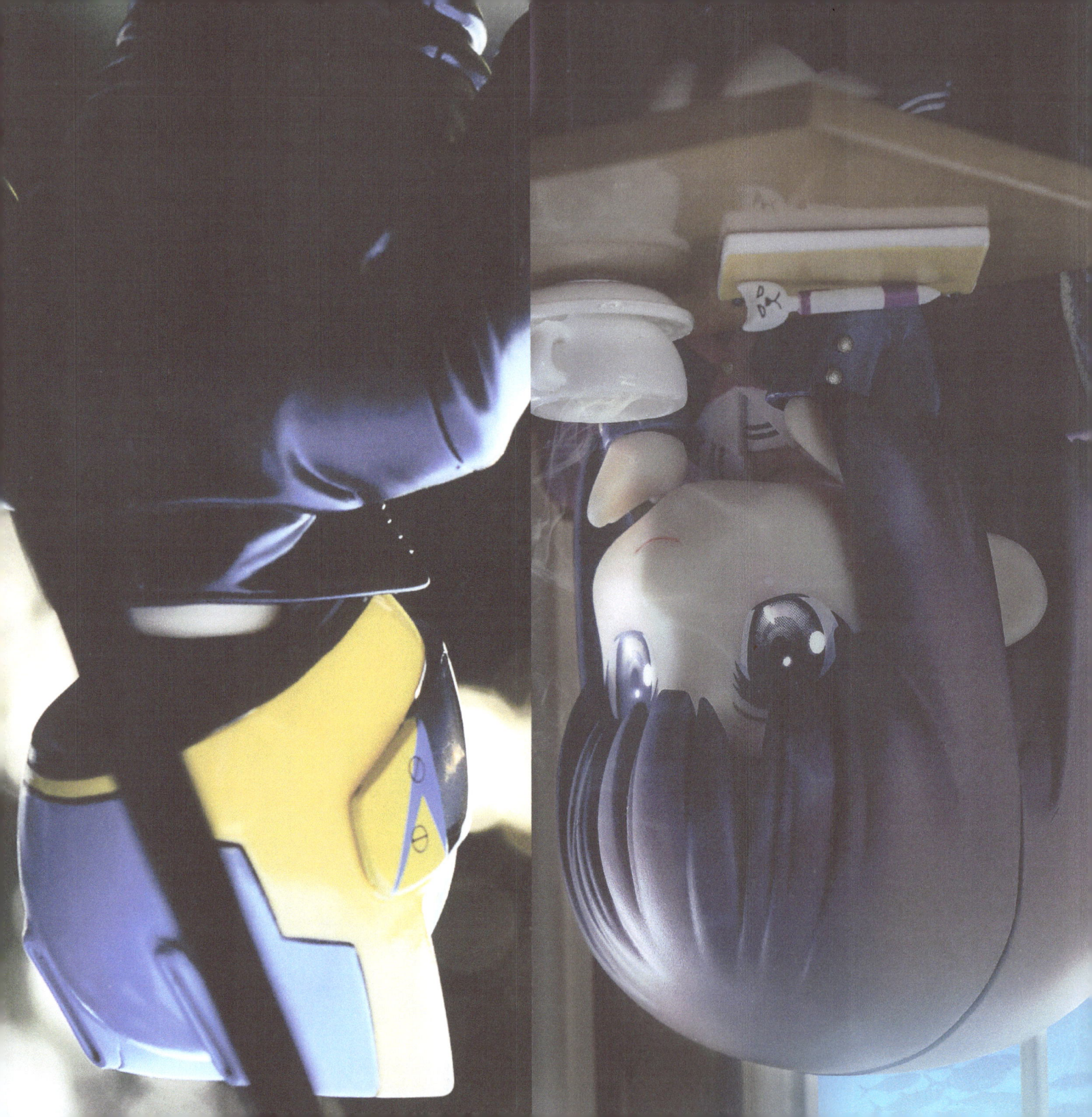

USA REGION: WEST

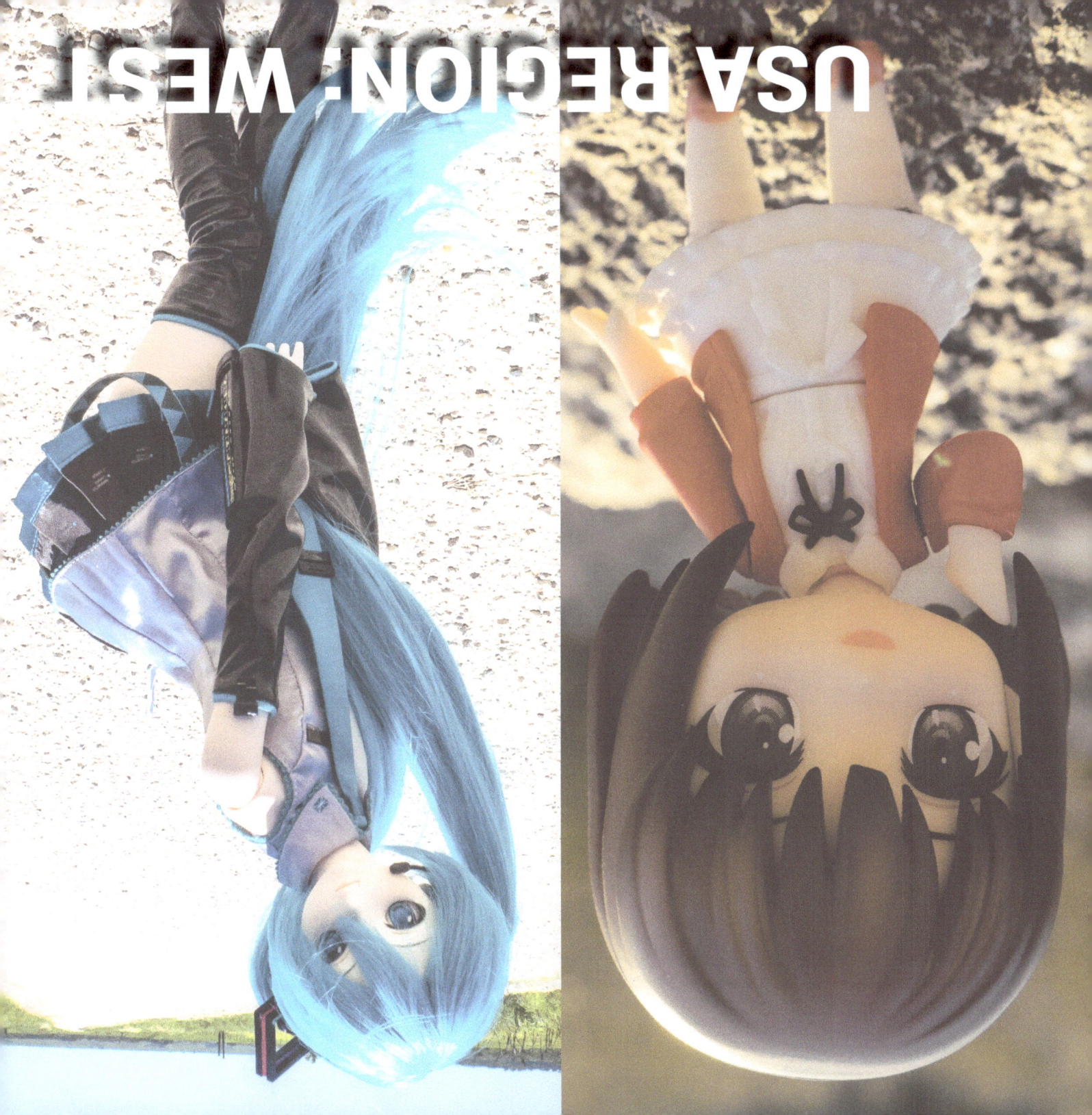

KENNETH BOLIDO

@KENBOLIDO @DAAIOSHI @KENBOLIDO HTTP://YOUTUBE.COM/FULLOANIME

St. Louis, MO

My name is Kenneth Bolido and I make videos on YouTube for a living. I've always loved filming stuff, so when I got into anime and figures 5 years ago, I knew I wanted to create content around my new hobby. Up until a few years ago, much of my time was spent on the fullOanime FigureSpotlight video project, which was featured and commissioned by Good Smile Company and Kotobukiya to showcase figures to fans around the world. Currently I am the lead producer for the Austin Evans tech YouTube channel.

When I was approached about working on this photobook, I was moving cross-country from New York to California. Normally, my videos are shot using carefully controlled diorama sets, so this was the perfect opportunity to step outside my comfort zone to photograph exclusively outdoors.

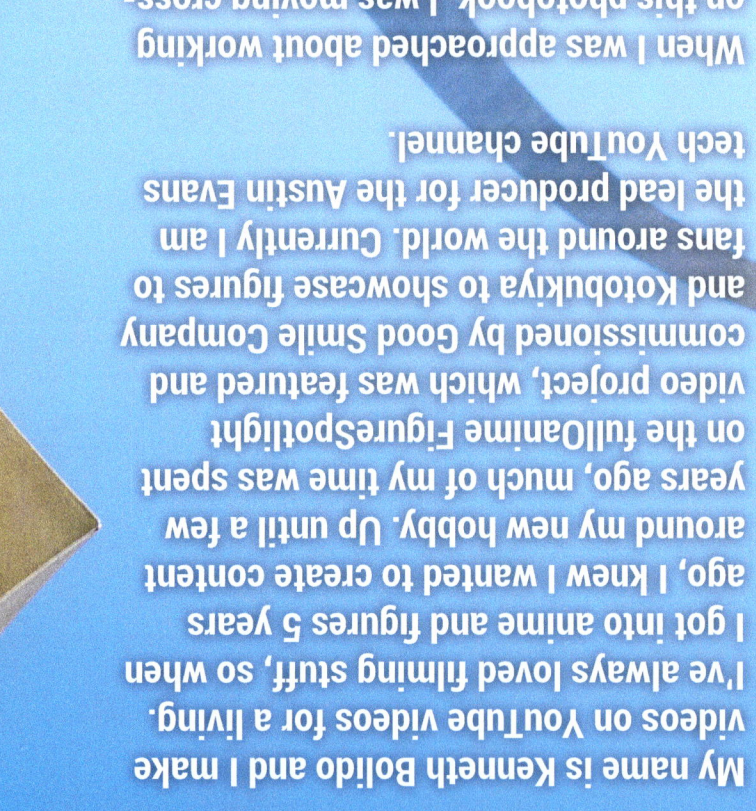

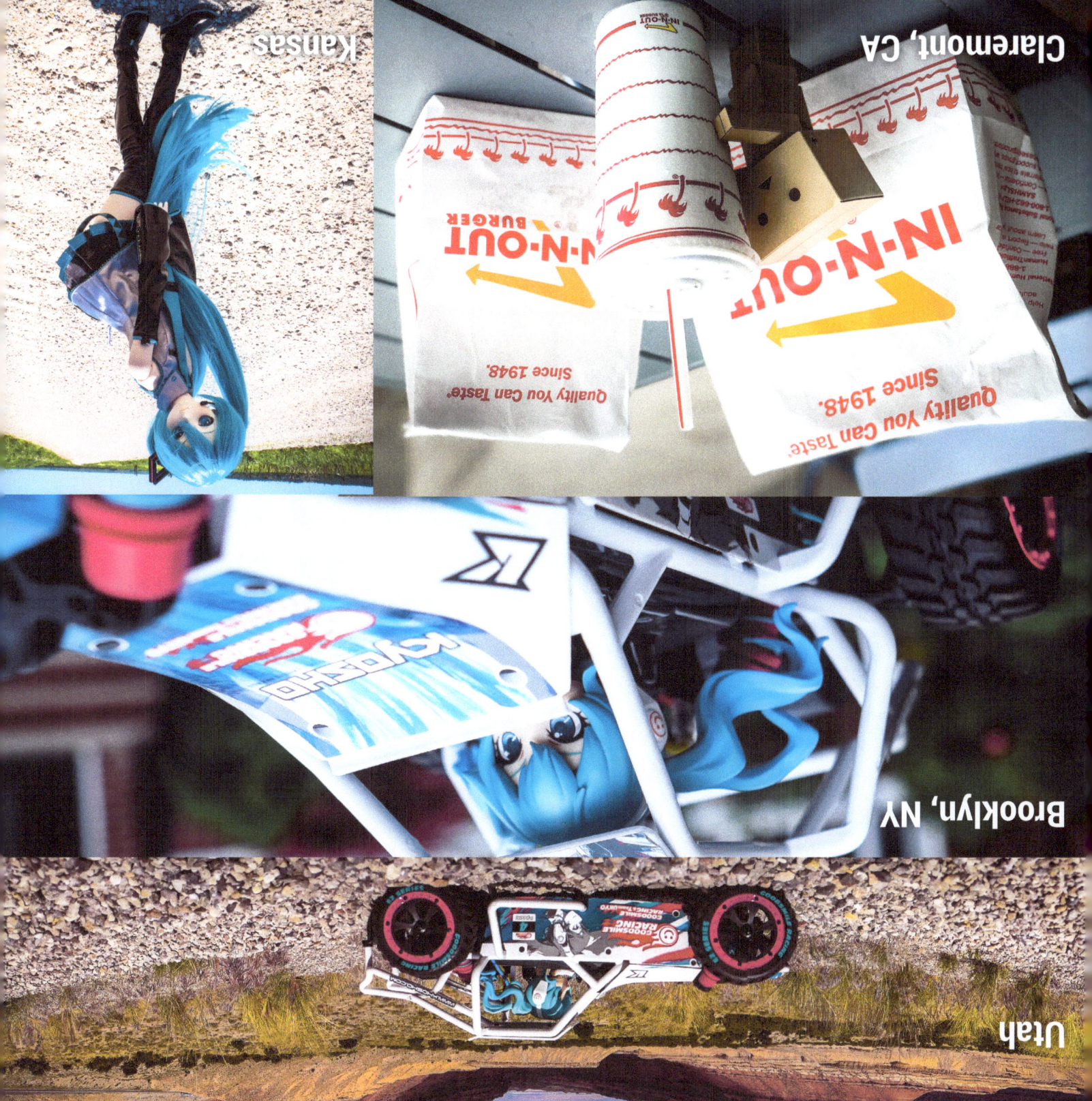

THEBEARDEDBAKA

@THEBEARDEDBAKA

Hi! I'm TheBeardedBaka. I've been photographing and collecting for a few years now. Originally started collecting figures to help with me get comfortable with portraiture photography but it quickly became a thing of its own! I honestly don't think I'd be as big of a fan of figures were it not for the photography aspect and the figure photo community. Apart from figure photography, I enjoy street, architecture, and landscape photography as well.

Arizona is well known for its exhausting dry heat but that doesn't we're unable to enjoy our time outside. There are several different hiking and walking trails all around the Phoenix area. I decided to showcase all of the nearby nature.

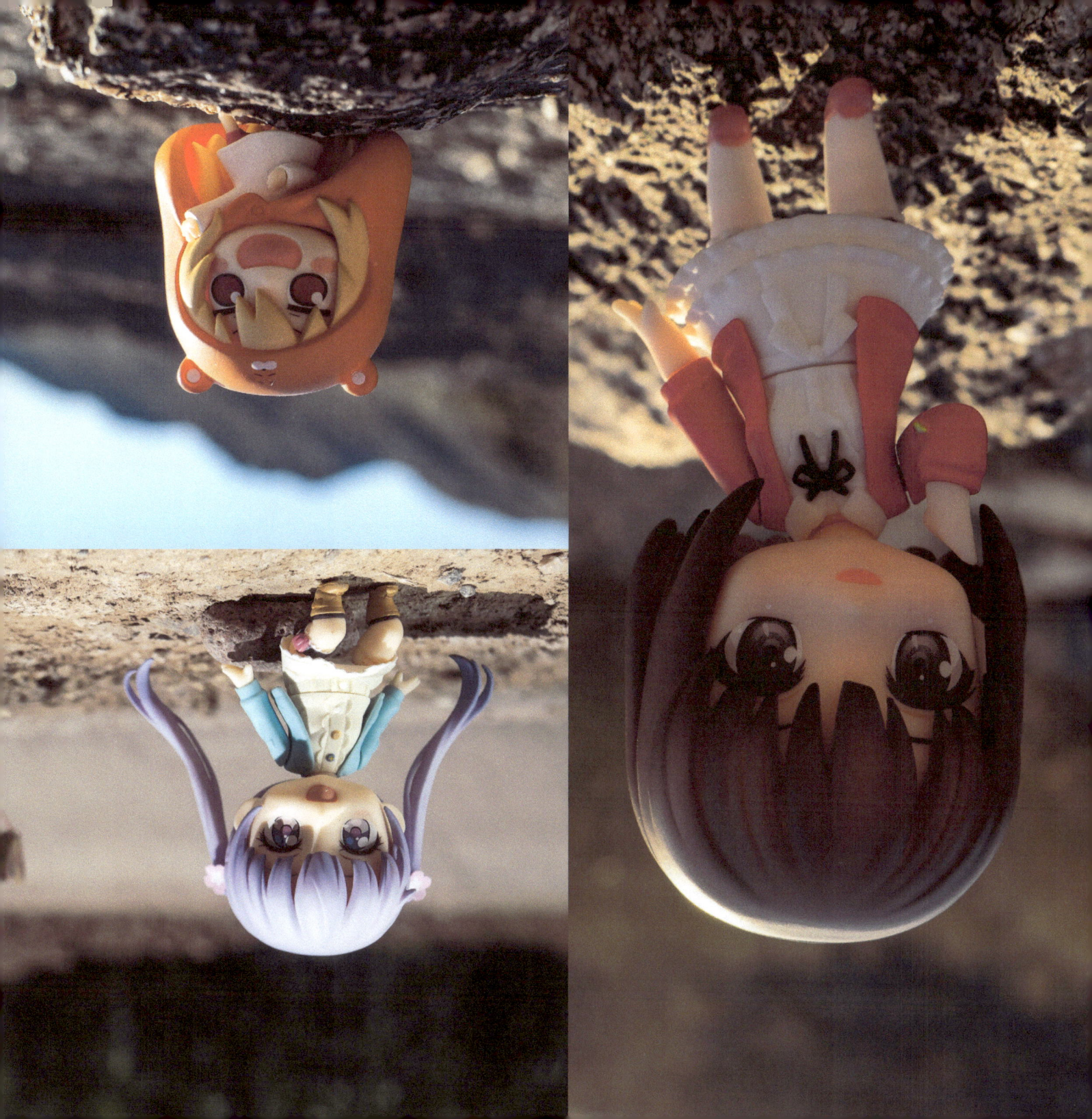

85CMPERSECOND

 @85CMSQUIDDO
 @85CMPERSECOND

Hi, I'm Julie! I've been doing amateur toy photography for a few years now, but I started casually collecting figures about 6 or 7 years ago. I used to only collect a few things, but I watched Madoka Magica and the character designs and appeal of a magical girl team' definitely sucked me into the figure hobby completely... I'm glad I fell into it though, the toy photography community is so lively and interesting!

I live in California, in a small community in the countryside, so that's why my photos tend towards nature themes. Also, Disney is another hobby of mine, so I like taking a few small figures to Disneyland for photos when I go for a visit!

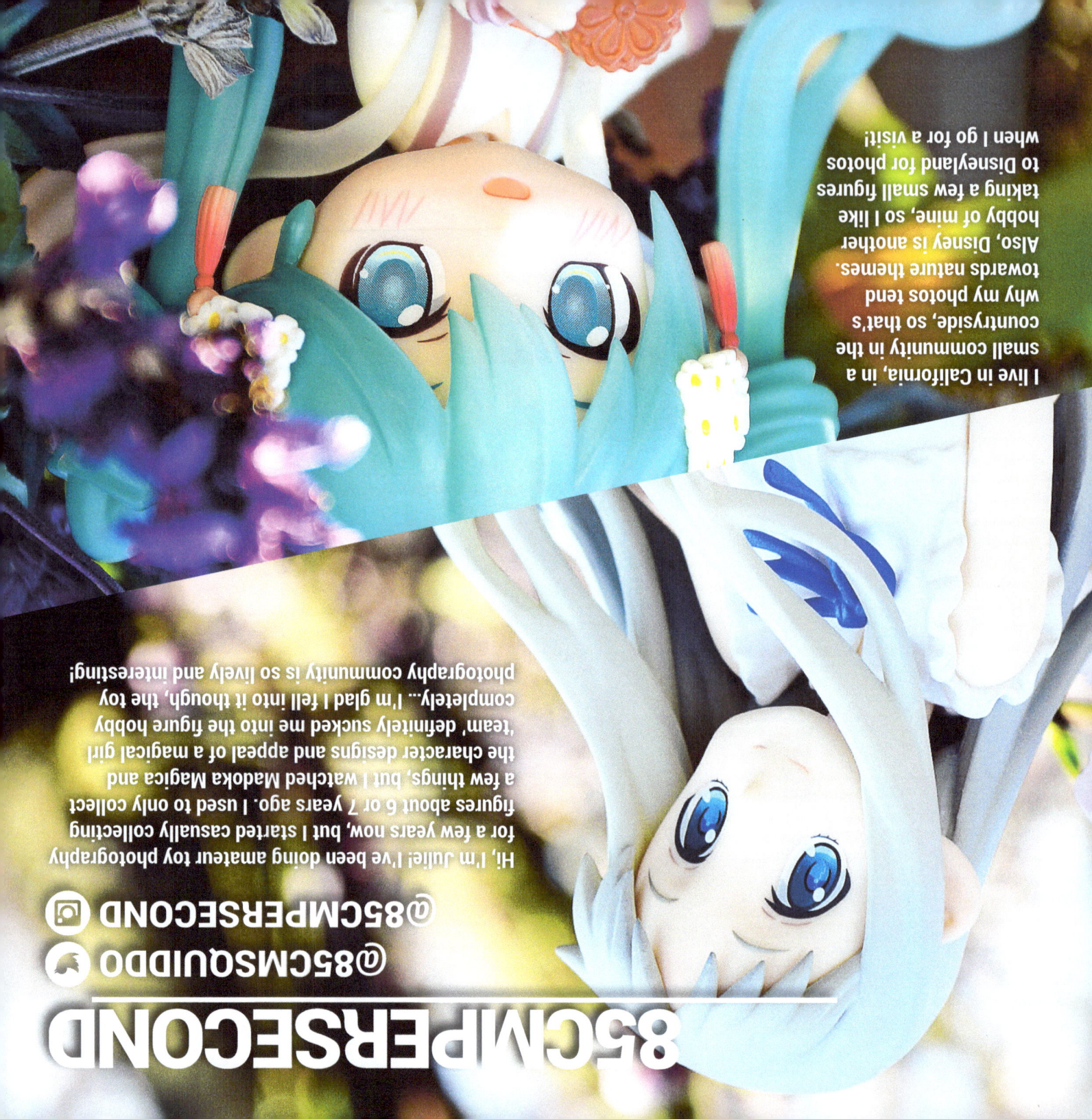

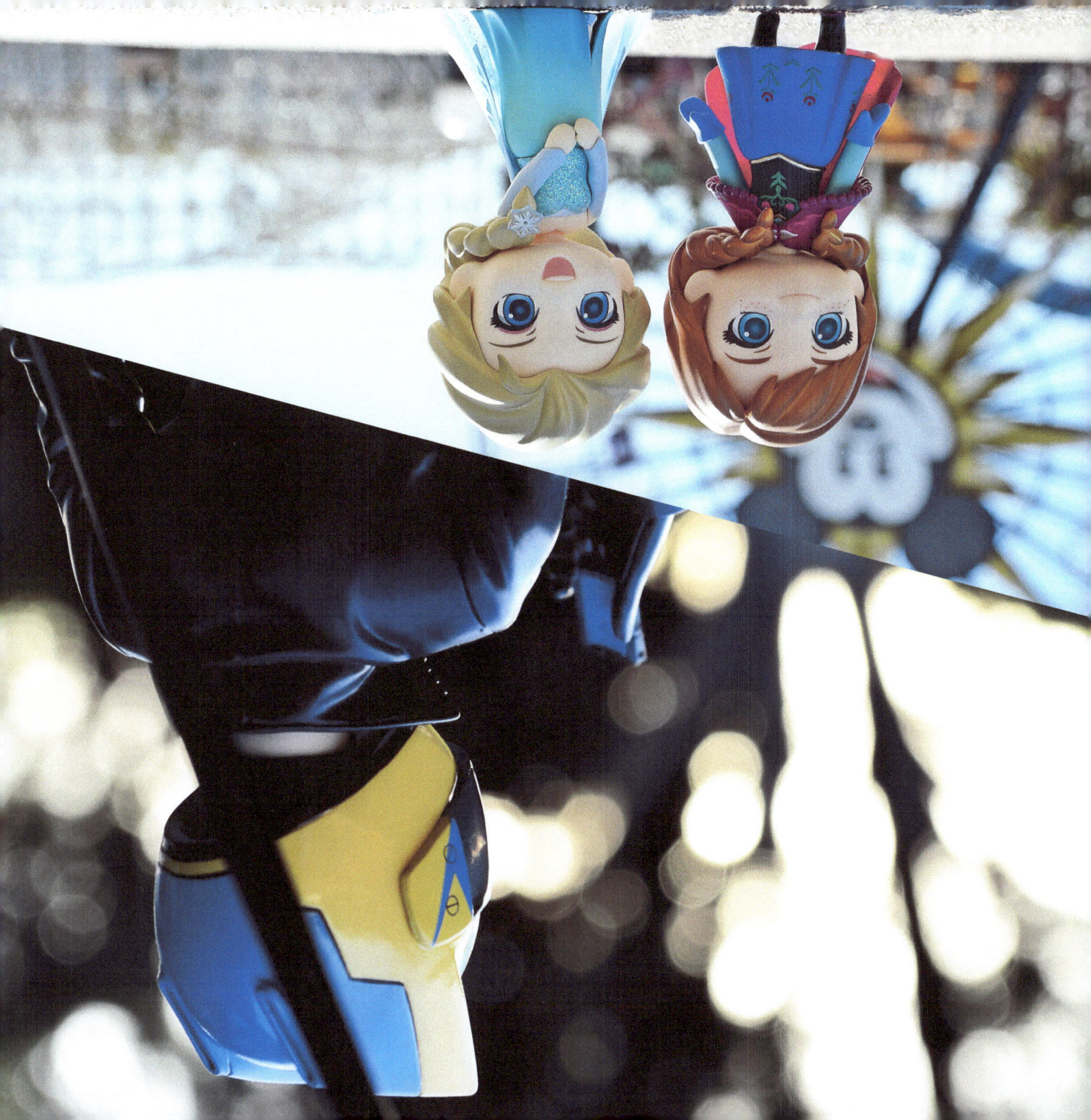

BALANCE
AKA REPRISE PHOTOGRAPHY

 @IGFXBALANCE

 @reprisephotography   reprisephotography.com

Hello, I am Balance! Back when I used to attend the Art Institute, I had a photography class that required a purchase of a DSLR. I ended up getting the Nikon D5100 kit from Costco. While the class was helpful, I was only given the bare minimum instructions on how to operate my DSLR. Later around 2013, I got my first nendoroid, Aozaki Aoko. I didn't do much with it until 2014 when I decided to try to use my camera more and try to take at least one picture every day of the year. When I discovered the toy photography community on Instagram, I found myself becoming more immersed into collecting figures and taking pictures! Ever since then, I've become more and more interested in photography and eventually translated those skills into portrait/cosplay photography.

I live 40 minutes south of Seattle, but still within the "Pacific Northwest" area most people are often familiar with when visiting Washington State. There's never a place where there are no trees and parks are abundant. Although living in WA usually means having to deal with 9 months of grey weather, it also means we often get 3 months of absolutely beautiful weather. It's always worth staying here in the end and I wouldn't want to live anywhere else.

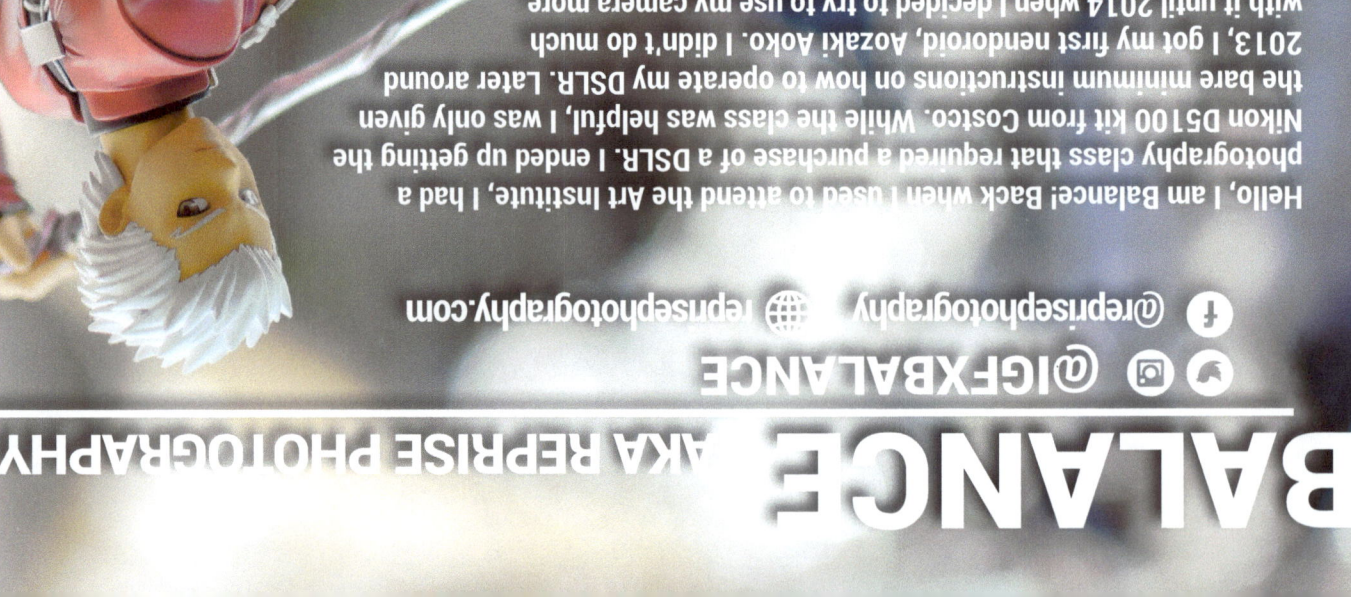

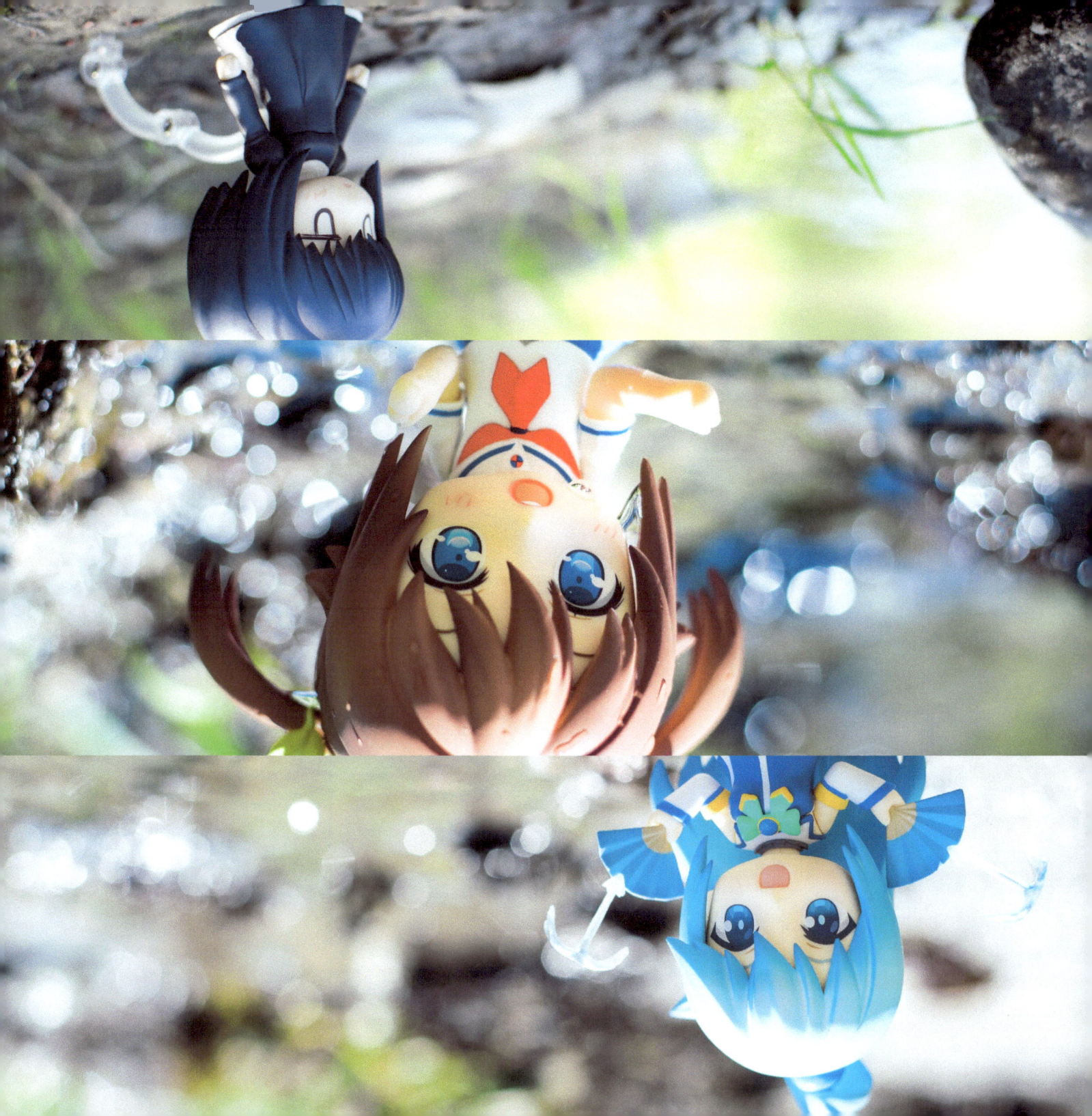

THE TRAVELING SEE

@thetravelingsee · myfigurecollection.net/profile/TheTravelingSee

Hello, I am TheTravelingSee. I picked up figure photography around January 2018. At this current stage of my figure photography career, I am exclusively a nendoroid photographer, though that may change in the coming months. In the beginning, I actually didn't like nendoroids all that much. I thought that their bulbous heads and disfigured proportions were unappealing when set beside a finely crafted scale figure. However, upon discovering the work of nendoroid photographers from around the world, the fanciful and childlike wonder of the nendoroid implanted itself within my heart from that moment on. And although I knew nothing about photography at the time, my father was an avid hobbyist. He taught me enough to get me on my feet and I haven't looked back since!

I live in Southern California. It'd be rather difficult to sum up the whole of the Golden State in one photo, seeing as how so many regions of the state differ in both geographical and social make up. But I felt as though, despite this, the beach was likely the most synonymous location with which California could be related to, excluding the obvious landmarks. With hot winters and even hotter summers, a dip in the ocean is everything a Californian could hope for!

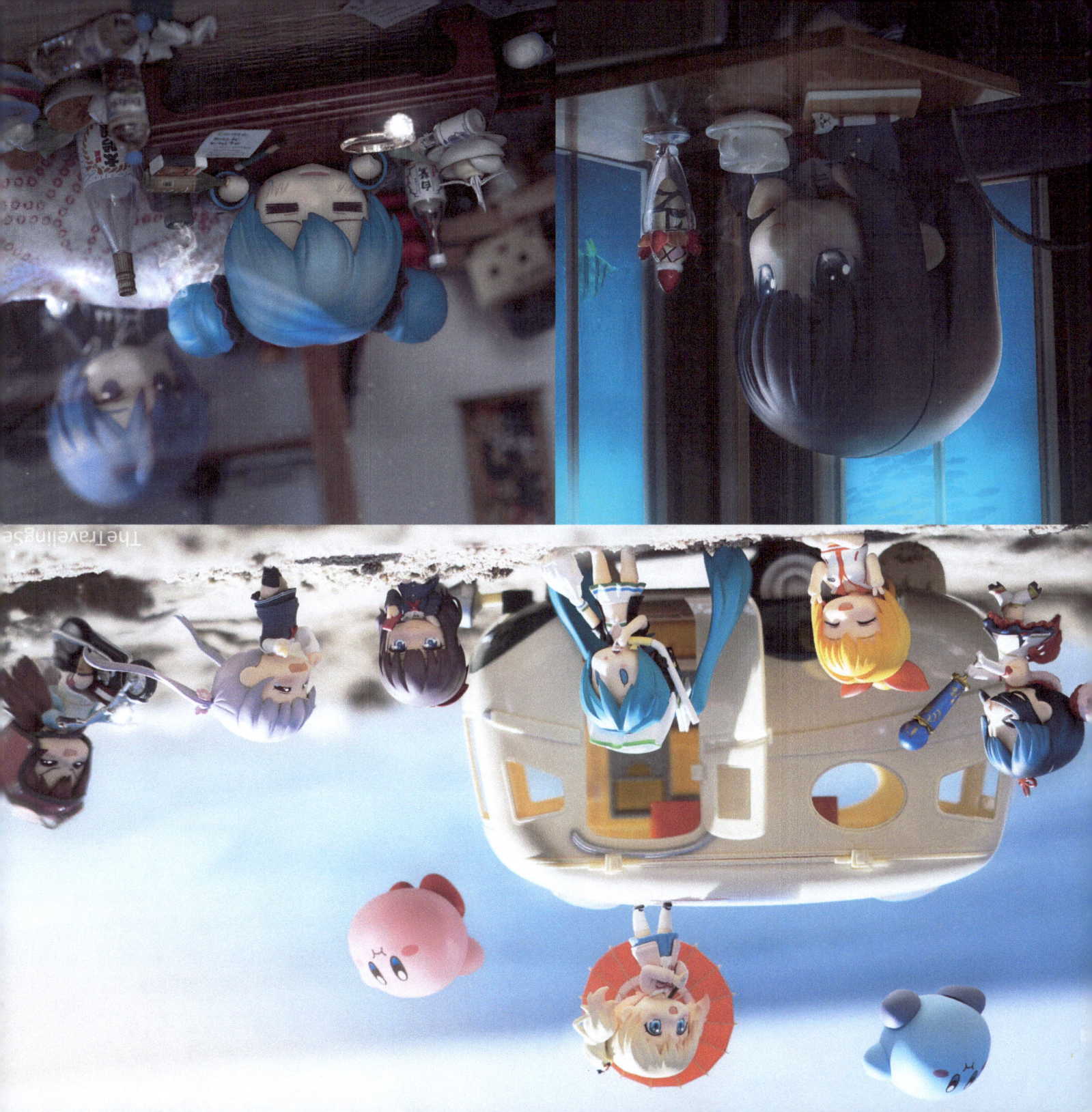

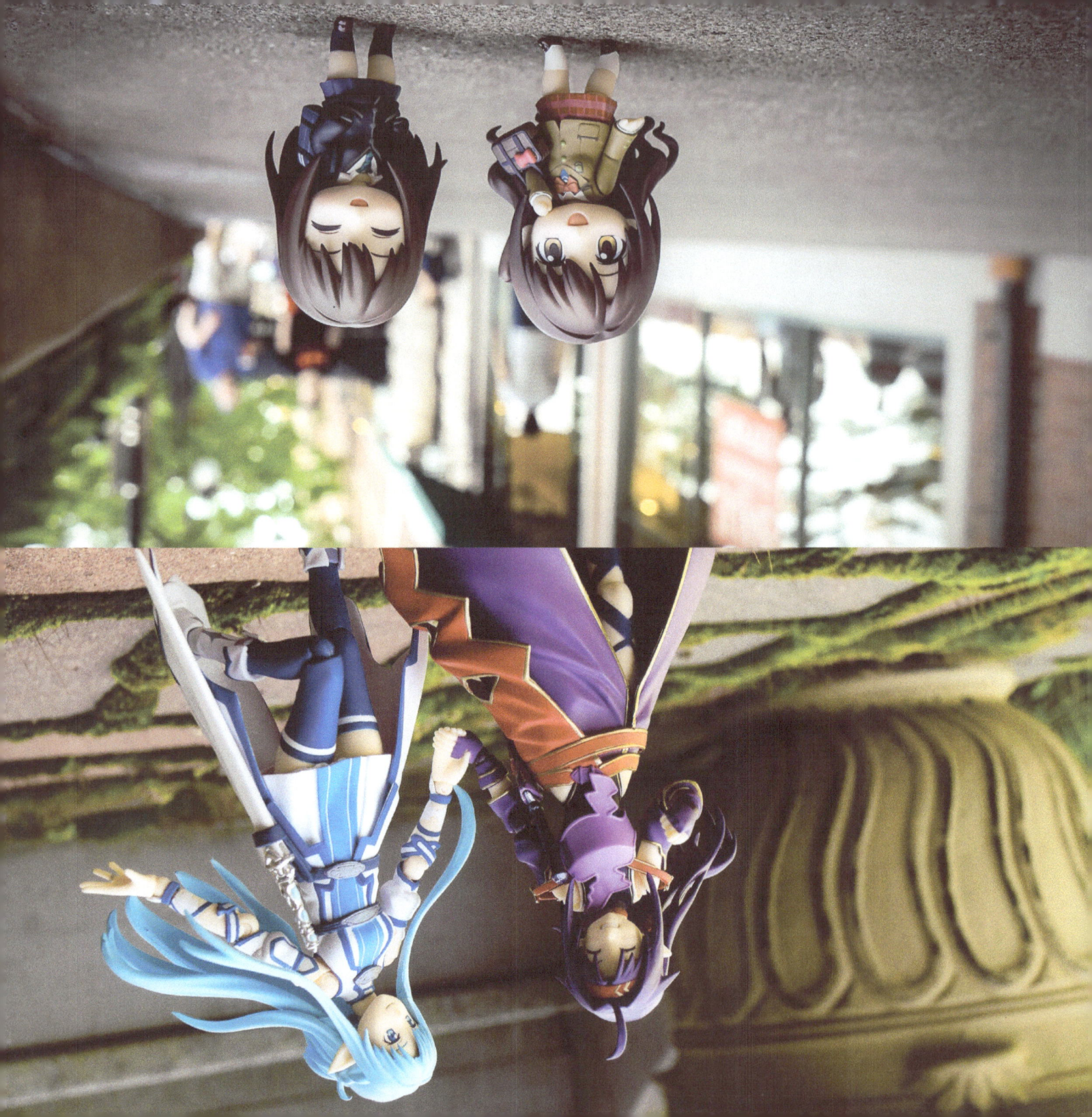

USA REGION: MIDWEST

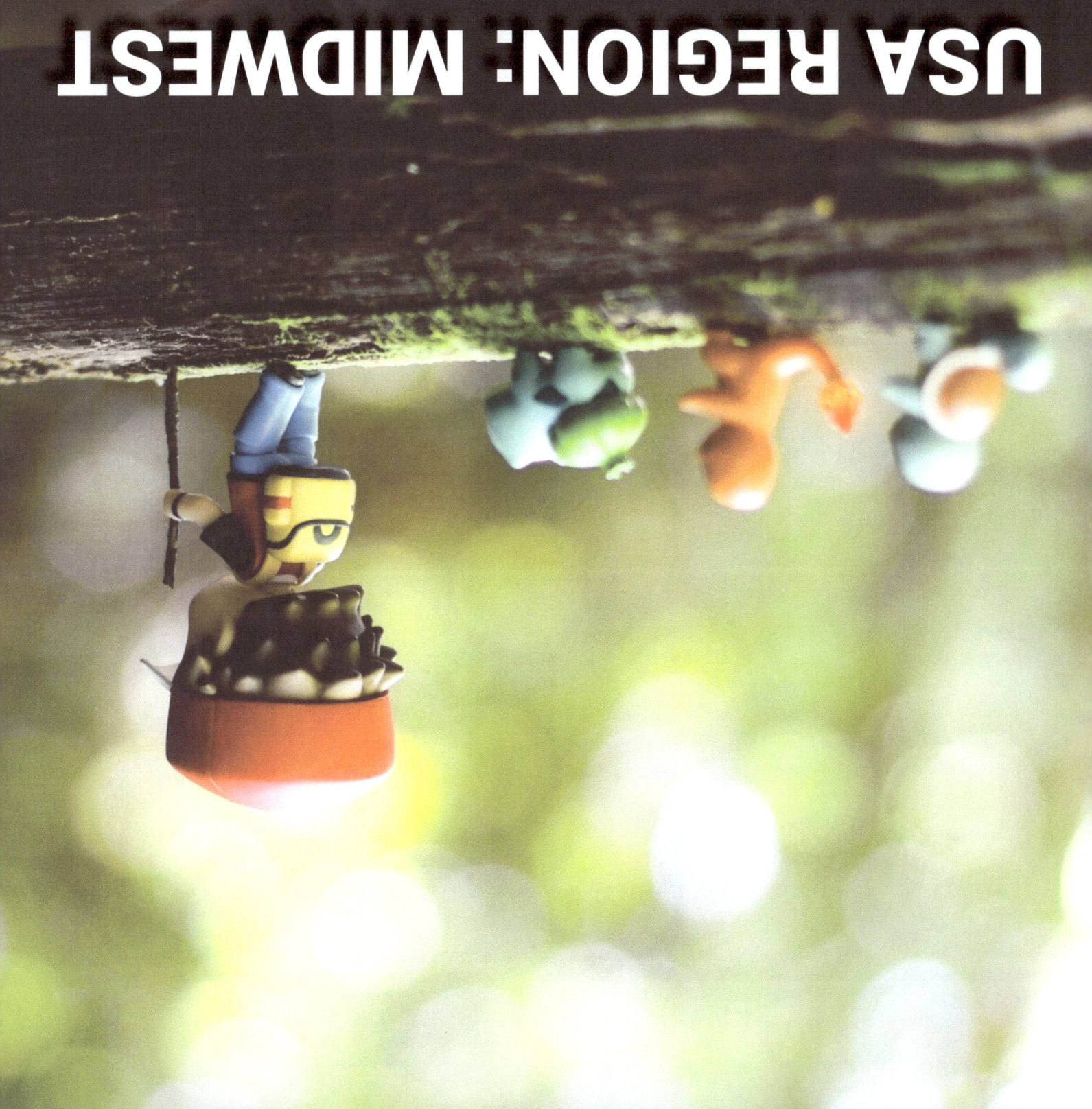

ISABEL (ICATTAILS)

🐾 📷 f @ICATTAILS
🌐 FLICKR.COM/ICATTAILS

Hello! My name is Isabel. Though I only recently started collecting figures (since 2014), I decided to take my passion one step further by photographing my collection. My favorite subjects are figma because of the challenges and opportunities they present from their poseability. Consequently, I tend to specialize in figma, though Nendoroids, action figures, and Gunpla also encompass my interests. It is an honor to be a part of this incredible community, and I hope you enjoy my work!

Oh, and just to settle the argument... FIGMA SUPREME!!

Minnesota: Land of 10,000 Lakes, wacky weather, and bustling metropolitan districts in the Twin Cities. This combination of the great outdoors and suburbia make my state special and exciting to explore.

In the fall of 2018, I moved to Los Angeles, CA.

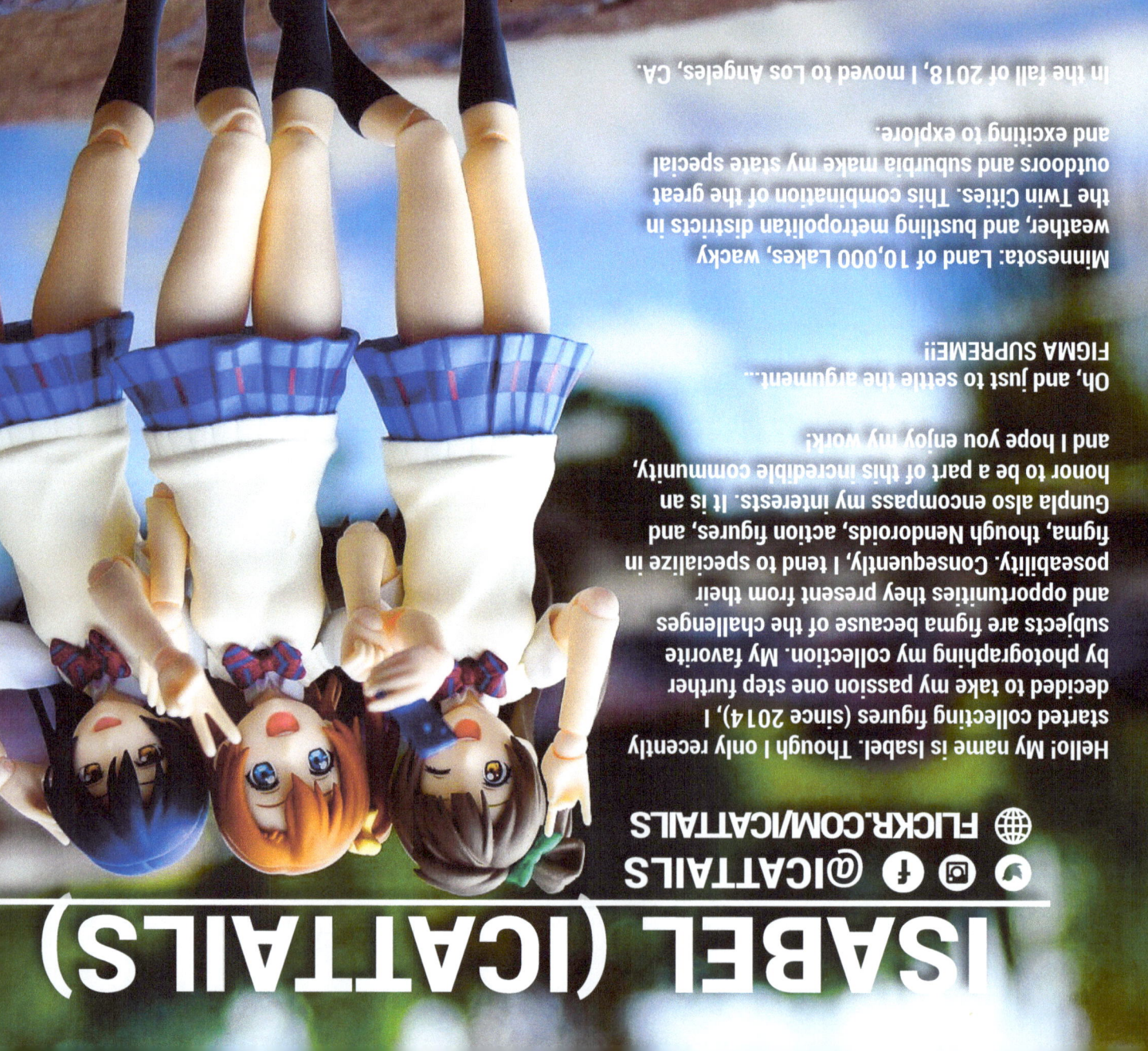

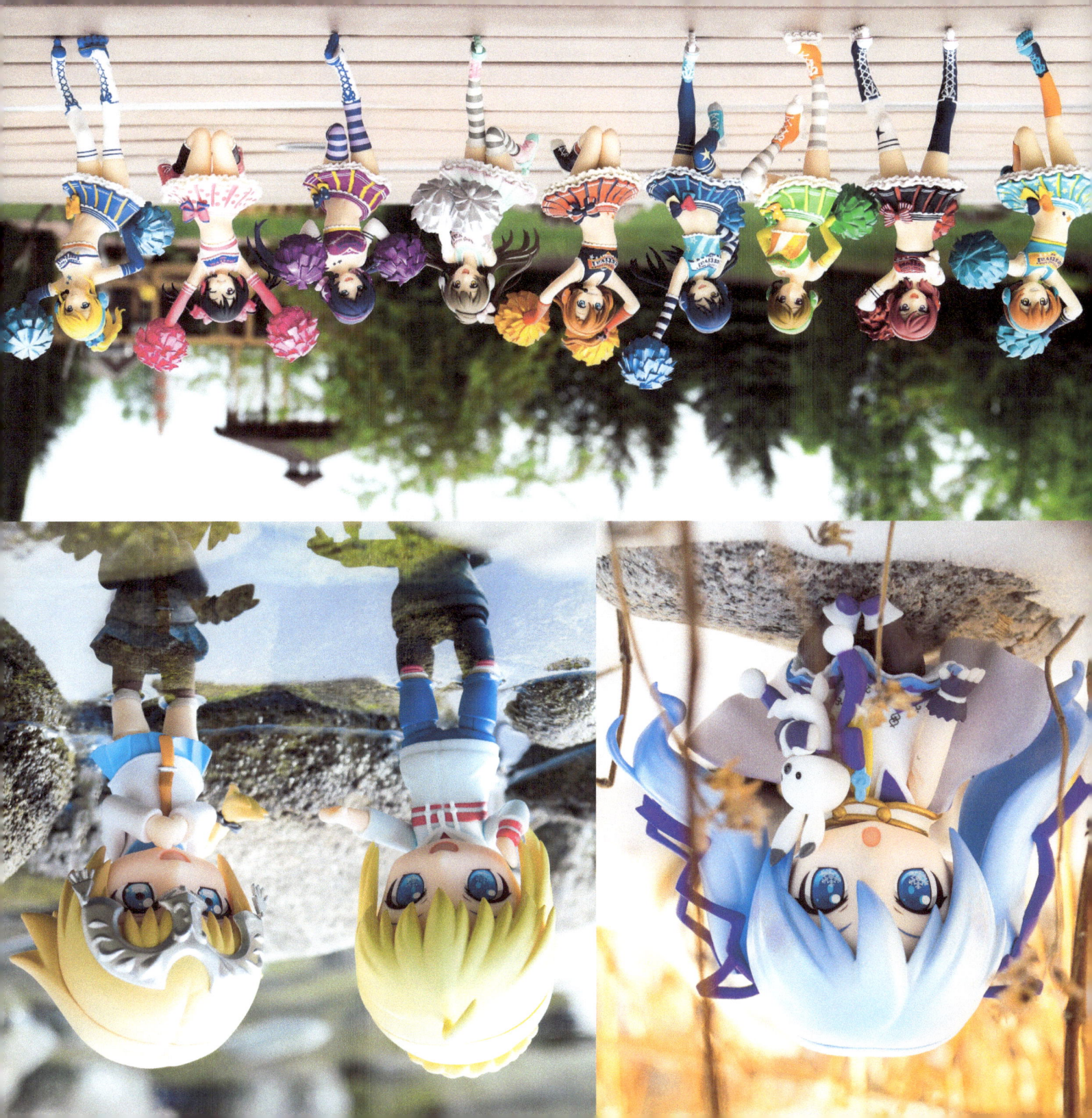

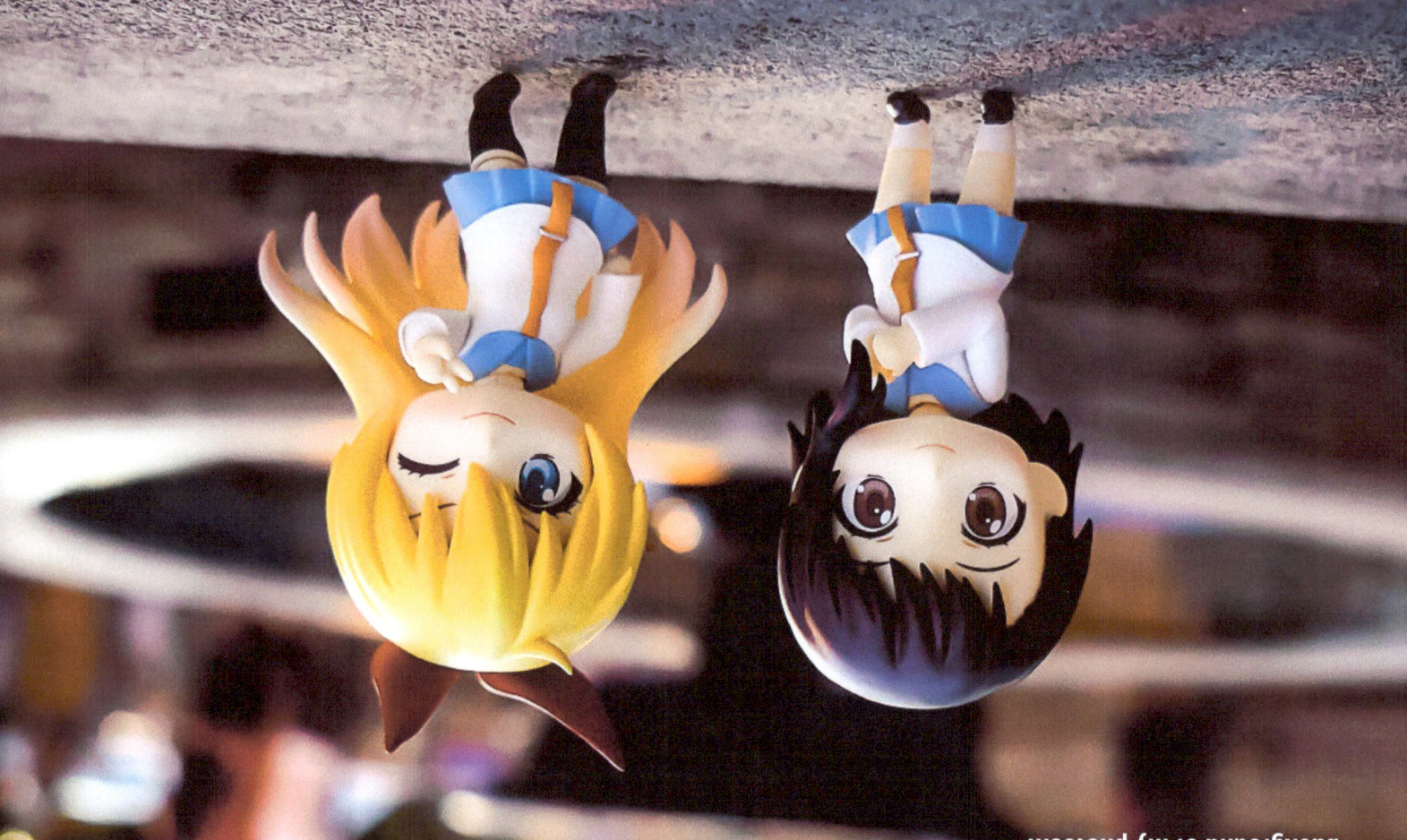

METANYANI

@METANYANI FLICKR.COM/METANYANI

Hello, I'm Philip also known online as either "meta" or "nyani", which I've combined into the name metanyani. I bought a camera purely for the sole reason of taking pictures of nendoroids, which I first started collecting in 2011. I'd describe myself as someone who's a huge fan of other figurine photographers more than actual photo taking myself. I just love being able to learn about the people are able to create imaginative and stunning figurine photos.

My photos were taken in my hometown of Naperville, which is one of the fastest growing cities in Illinois located west of Chicago. Many who visit say it has a small town feel. Naperville has a rapidly growing downtown shopping area and huge Riverwalk park to relax. It's always busy, and it's hard not to include people in the background of my photos...

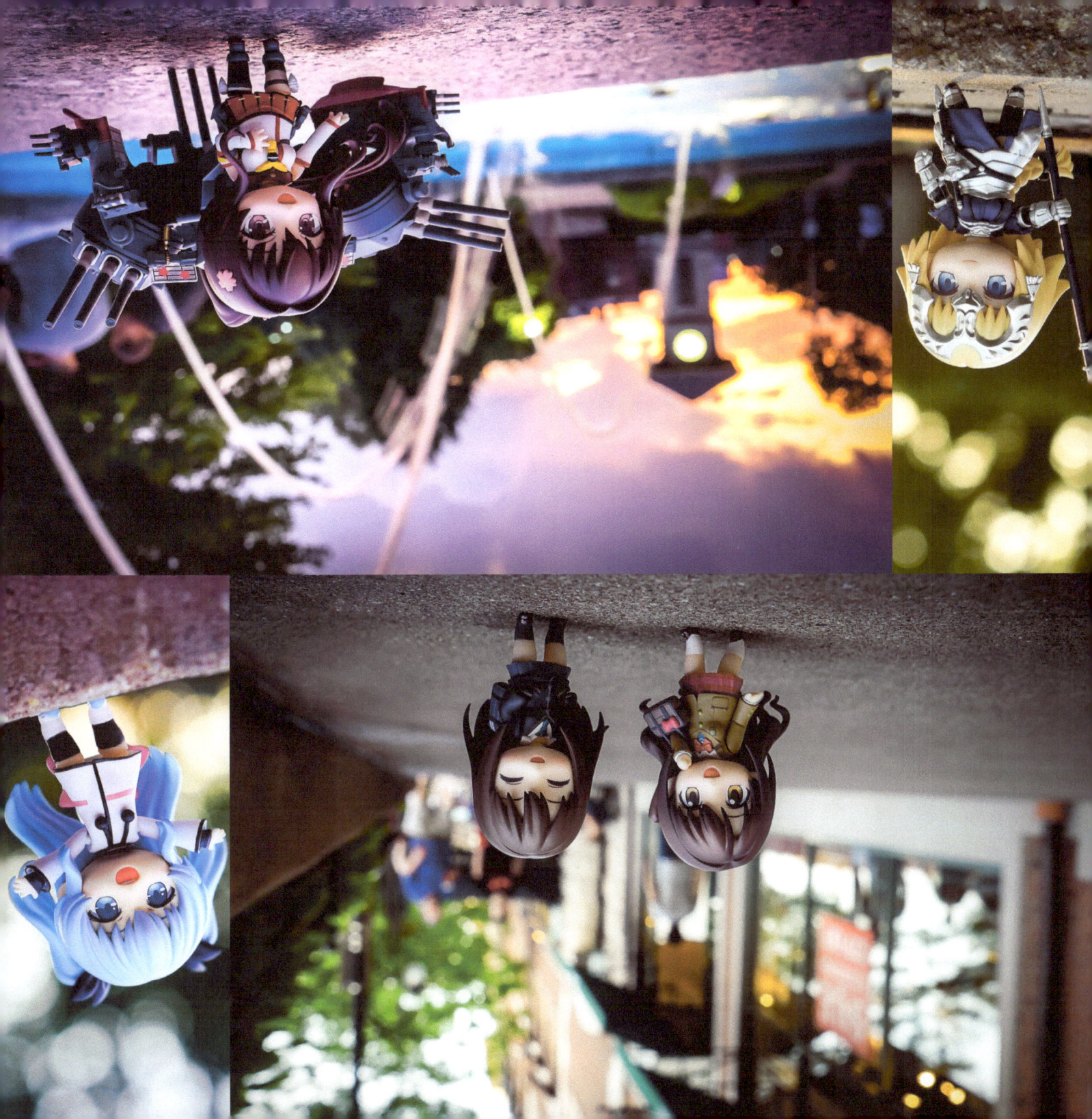

CAPTAIN DANGEROUS

 @CAPTDANGEROUS64   @DANG3ROUSPIX3LS   PATREON.COM/CAPTAINDANGEROUS   @CAPTAINDANGEROUS

Starting from an early age toys weren't toys. Her room wasn't simply a room. When crossing the threshold, you stepped into another world. To her, these figures stepped out of their universe and into hers. As she grew older the fervor for collecting and her creativity reached new heights.

Under the moniker CaptainDangerous, camera in hand, and slivers of what made her life so magical, she started to plow a path in the toy photography community.

She now works with Nintendo as a Brand Ambassador, VIZ media as a product photographer, and Tokyo Otaku Mode as a Special Creator.

Cincinnati, Ohio is surround by gorgeous hills and dense forests. There are so many beautiful parks and nature preserves to explore. While the weather can be extremely unpredictable here, it does make for a fun challenge when it comes to toy photography.

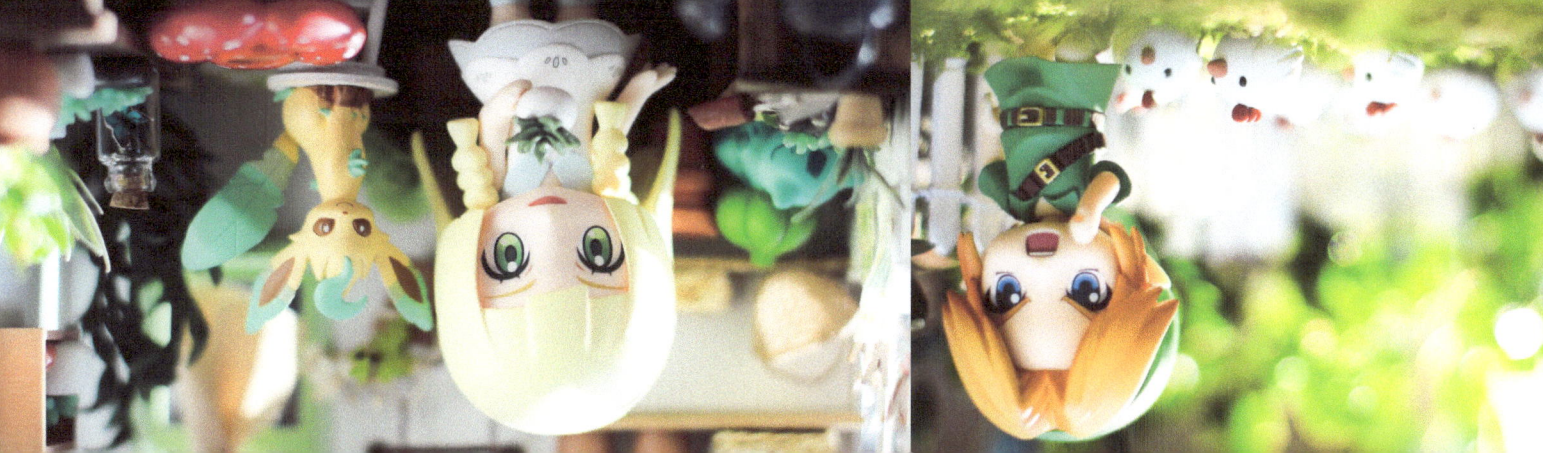

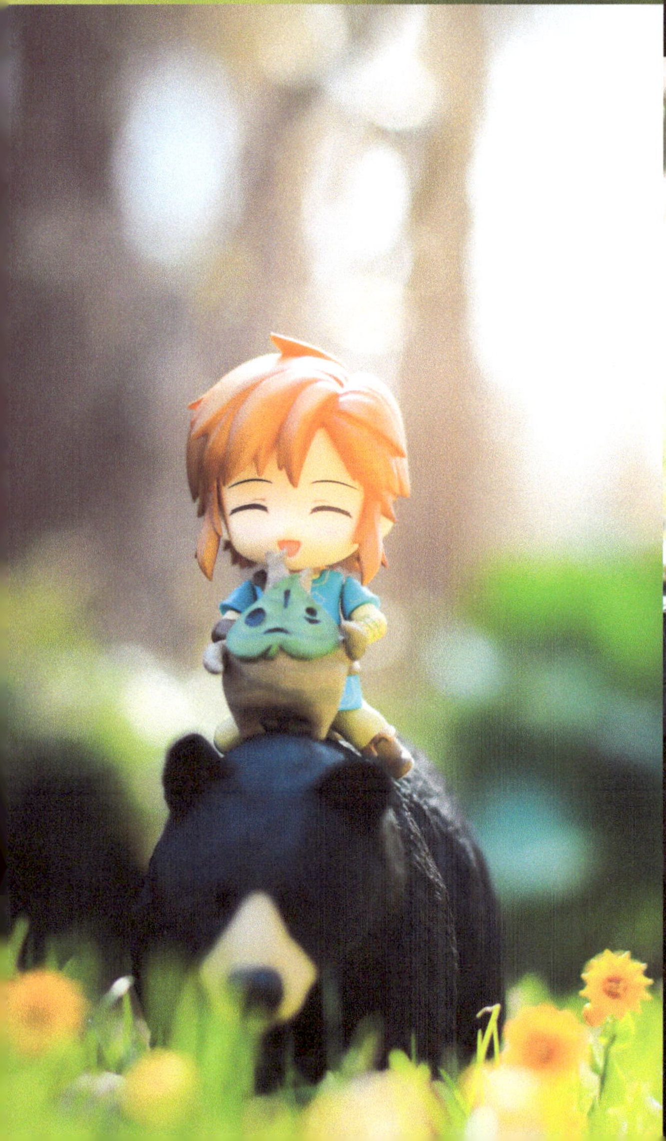

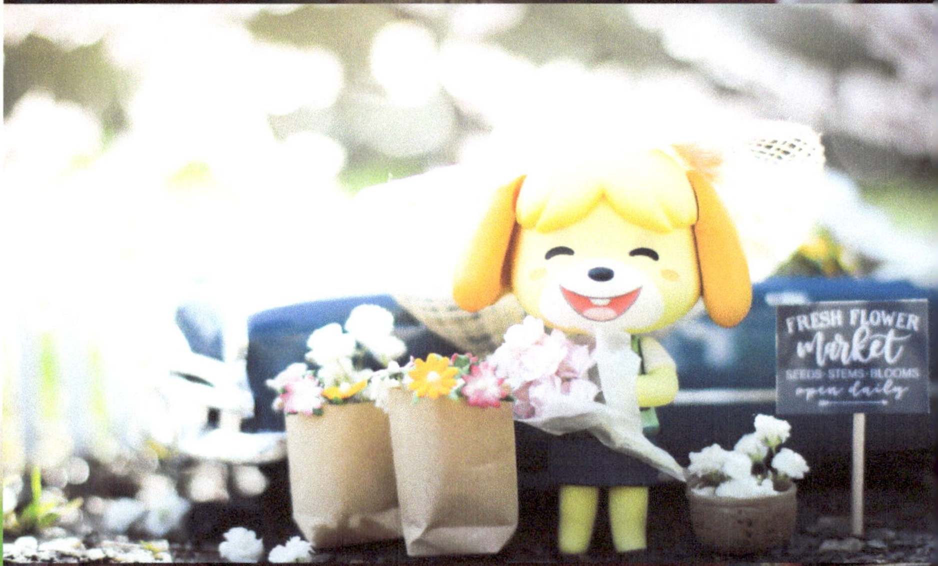

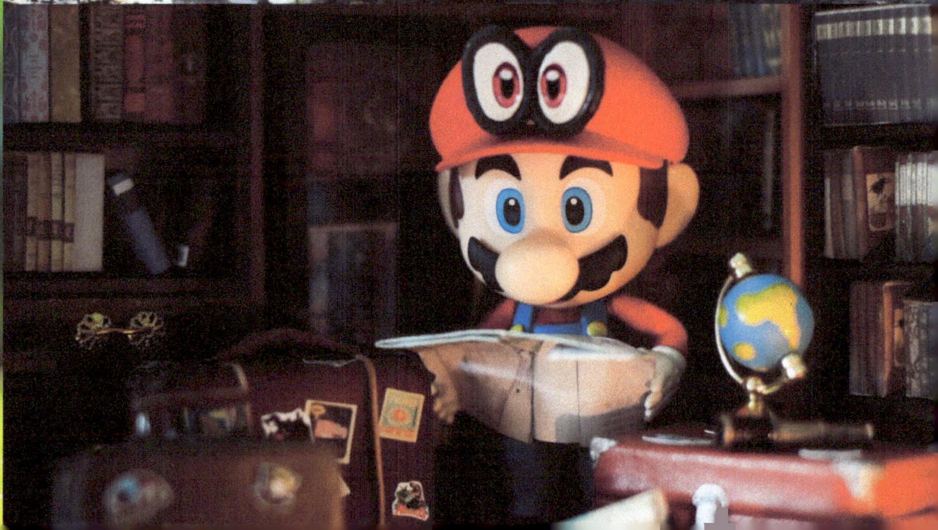

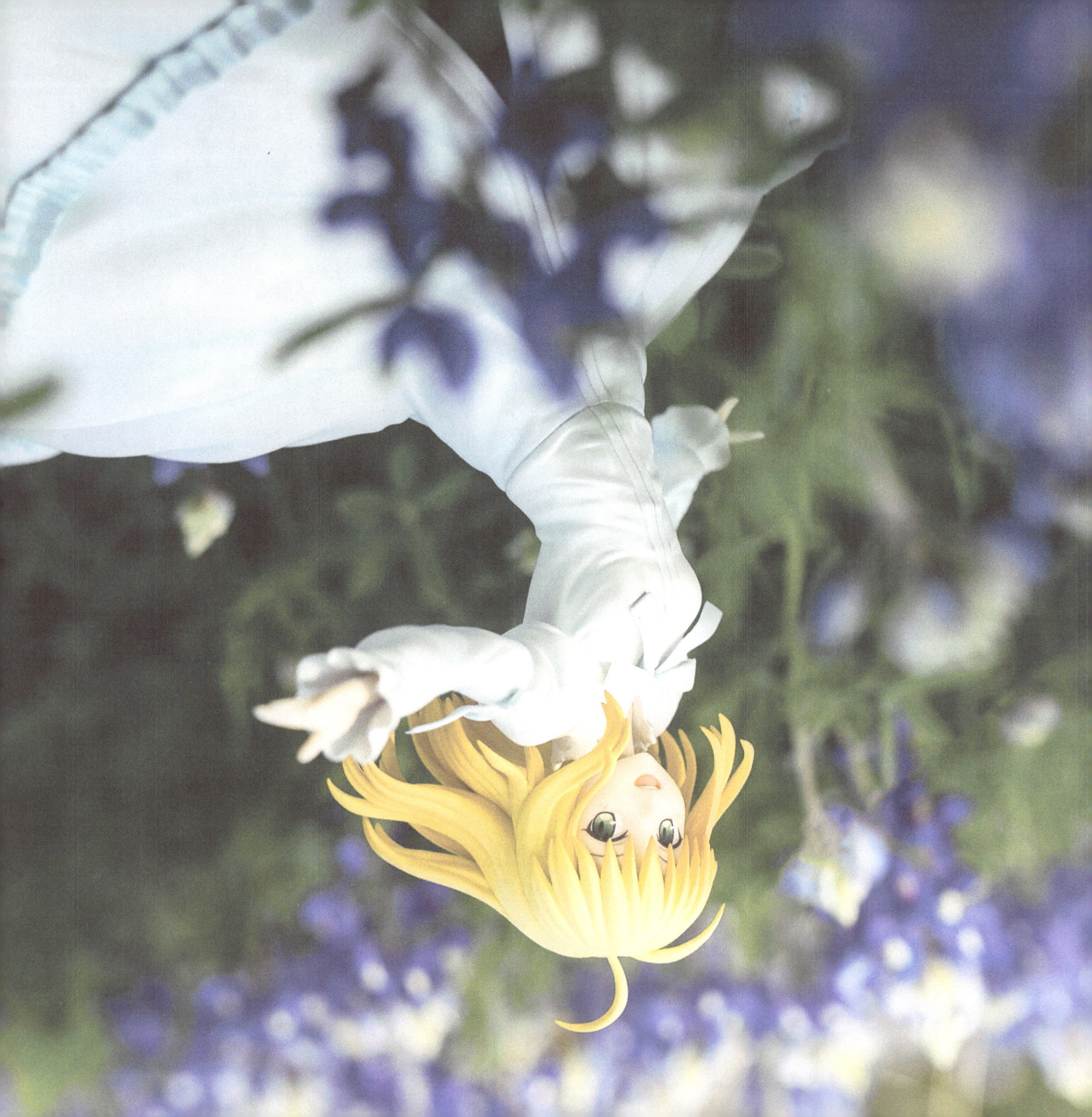

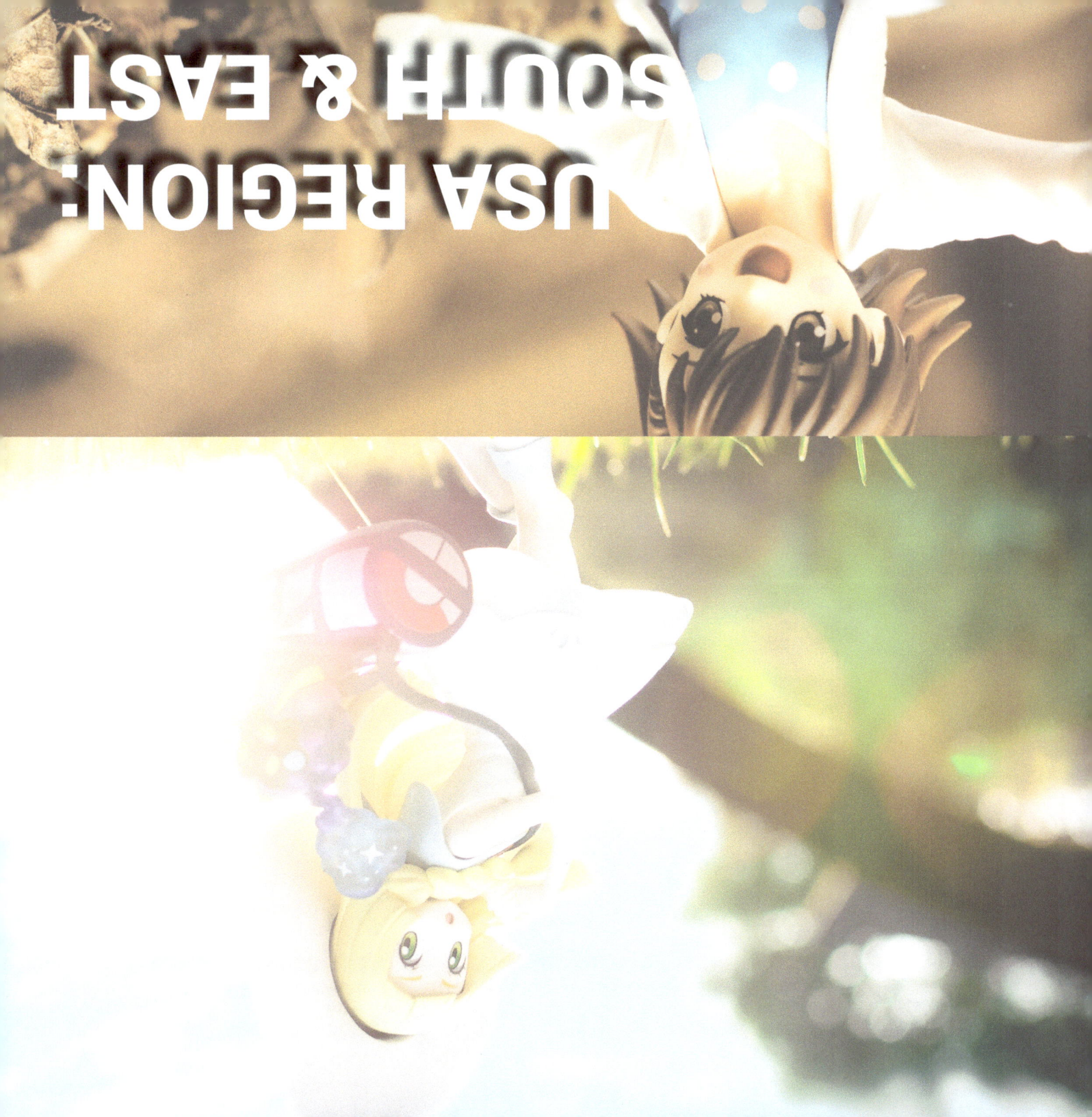

USA REGION: SOUTH & EAST

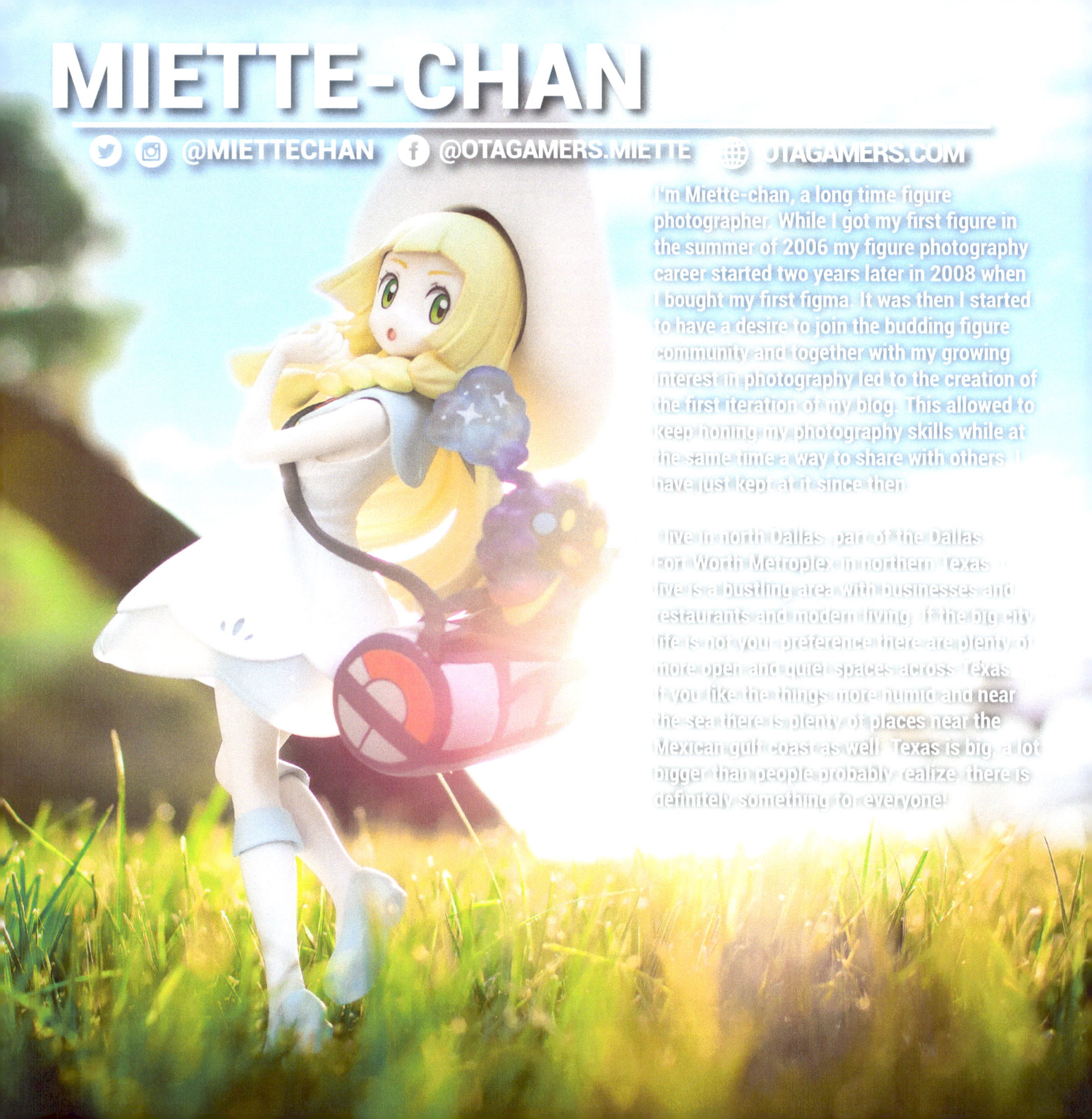

MIETTE-CHAN

 @MIETTE.CHAN @OTAGAMERS.MIETTE OTAGAMERS.COM

I'm Miette-chan, a long time figure photographer. While I got my first figure in the summer of 2006 my figure photography career started two years later in 2008 when I bought my first figma. It was then I started to have a desire to join the budding figure community and together with my growing interest in photography led to the creation of the first iteration of my blog. This allowed to keep honing my photography skills while at the same time a way to share with others I have just kept at it since then.

I've in north Dallas, part of the Dallas Fort Worth Metroplex in northern Texas. It's a bustling area with businesses and restaurants and modern living. If the big city life is for you, there are plenty of not open and quiet spaces across Texas. If you like the things more humid and near the sea there is plenty of places near the Mexican gulf coast as well. Texas is big, a lot bigger than people probably realize there is definitely something to everyone.

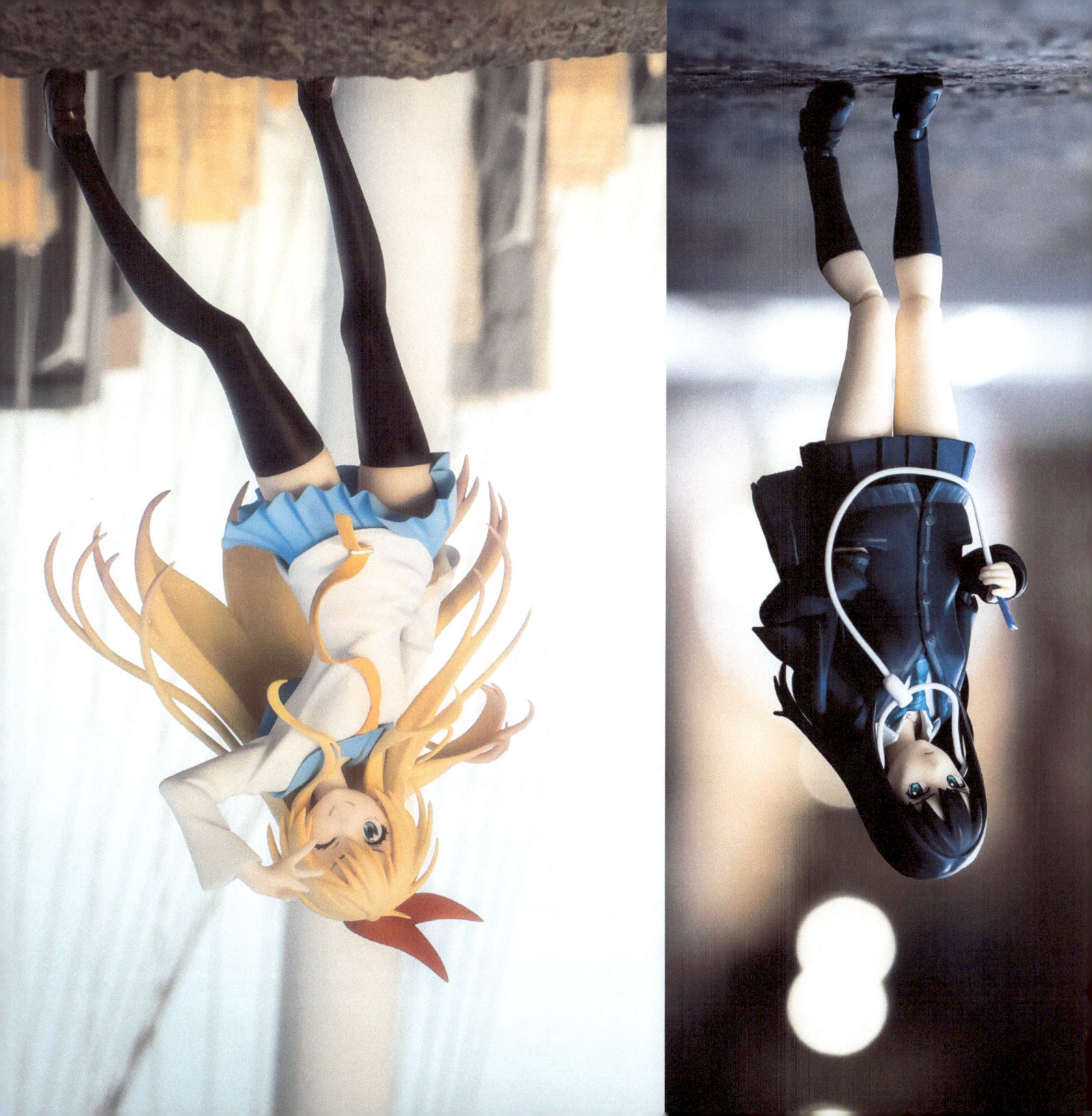

PENGUIN OTAKU PHOTOGRAPHY

📷 @PENGUINOTAKUPHOTOS

📘 @PENGUINOTAKUPHOTO

Hello I'm Mervin, but online I go by PenguinOtakuPhotos (a mouthful, I know). I've been collecting figures for about three years now, though I've only been taking figure photos seriously for eight months. My inspirations stem from Marco from AkibaCorner who gave me a lot of advice when I first started off along with a fellow photographer from this book Ken. Though the biggest influence that began this journey was with a social media app I once used called "Anime Amino". I was featured several times on the home page for my figure related blogs which eventually caused the biggest spark of inspiration to take figure photography more seriously.

The photos I took come from a variety of places in Pennsylvania and Maryland. These states are very heavy in nature and home to several historic locations. From the Gettysburg where one of America's most iconic speeches was given, to the graffiti rocks at High Rock Mountain in Maryland, back to the leaf covered trail in New Freedom. These locations may not always stand out, but when you take a moment, there may be more to appreciate than you first noticed.

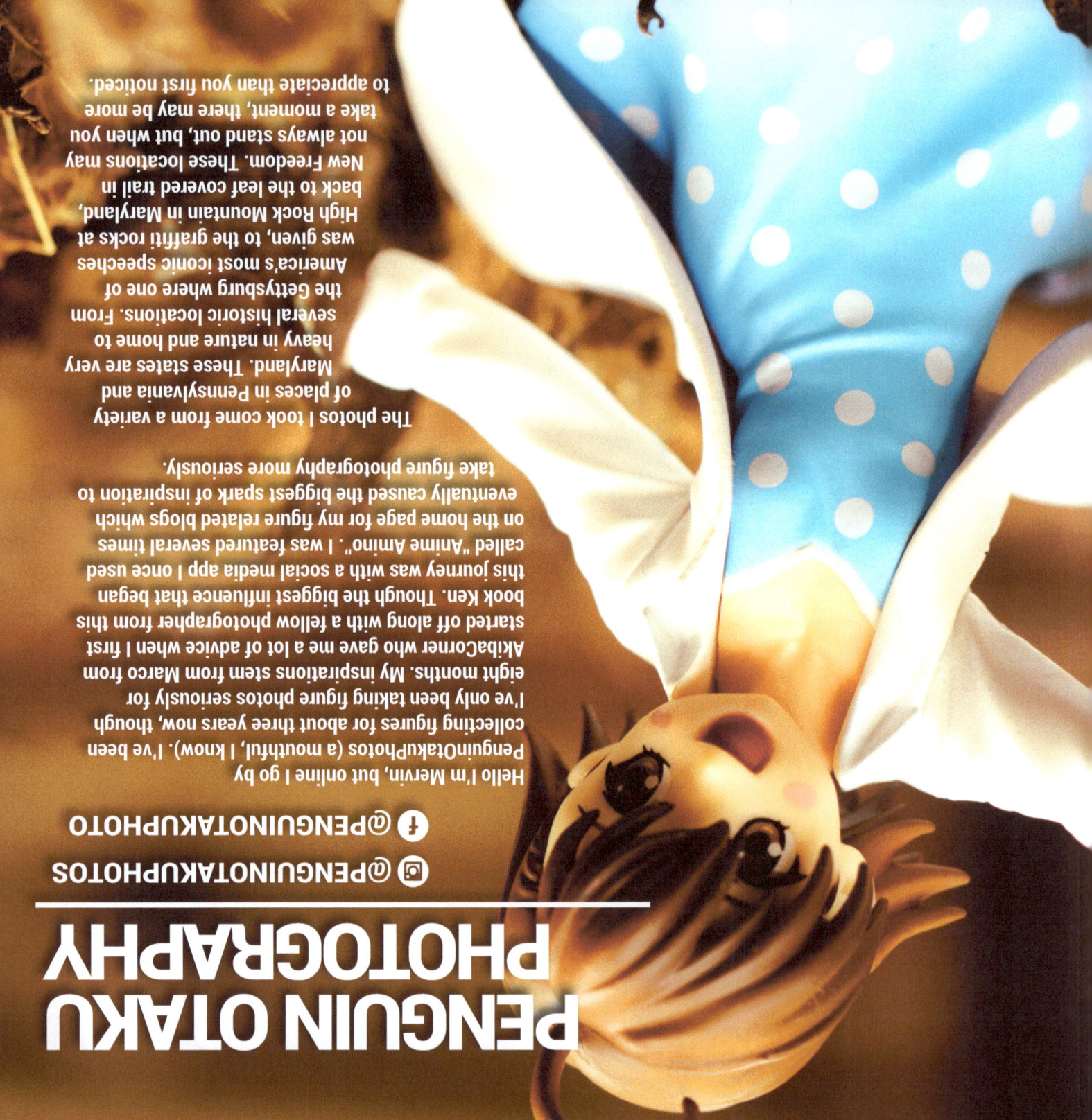

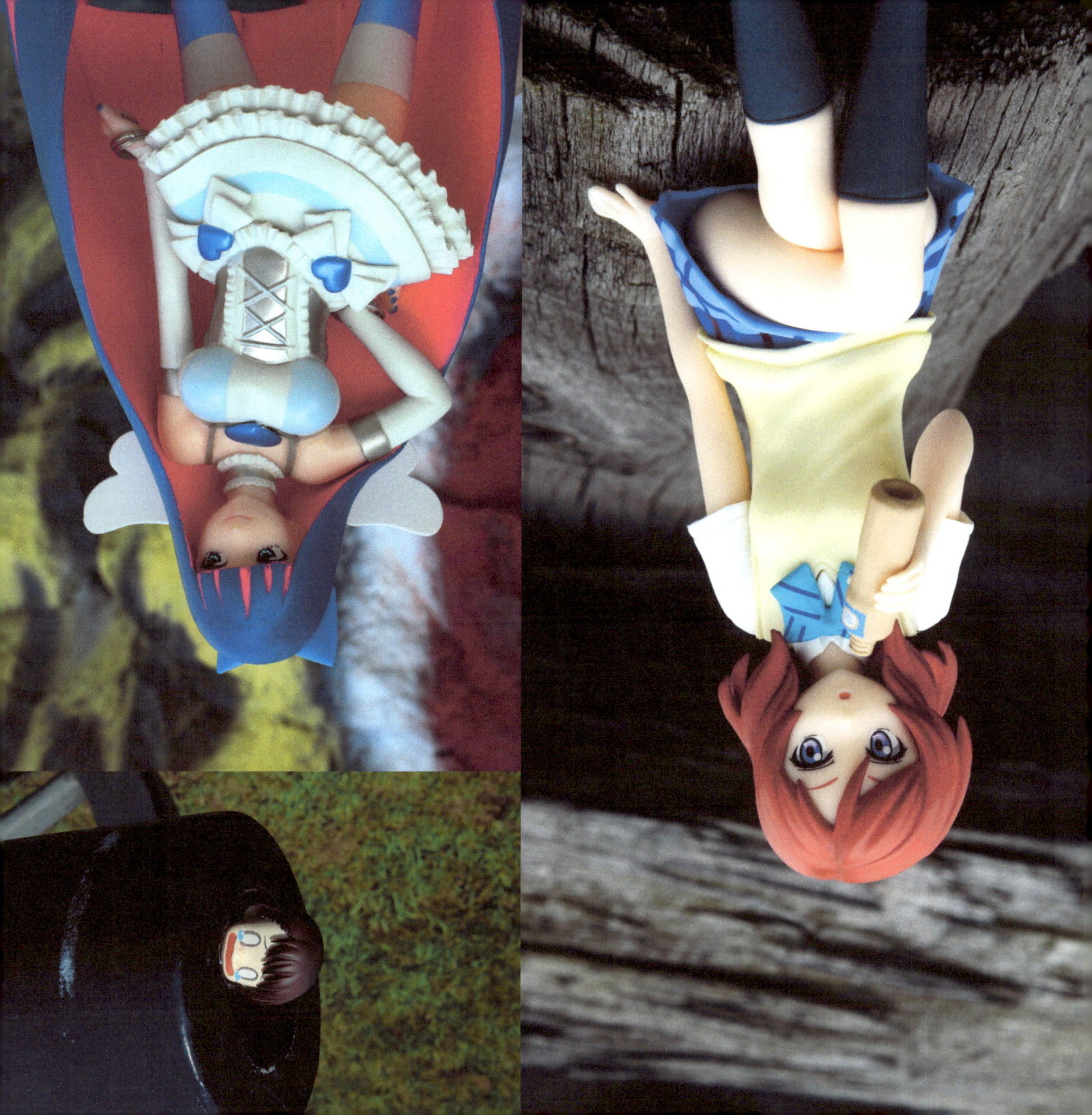

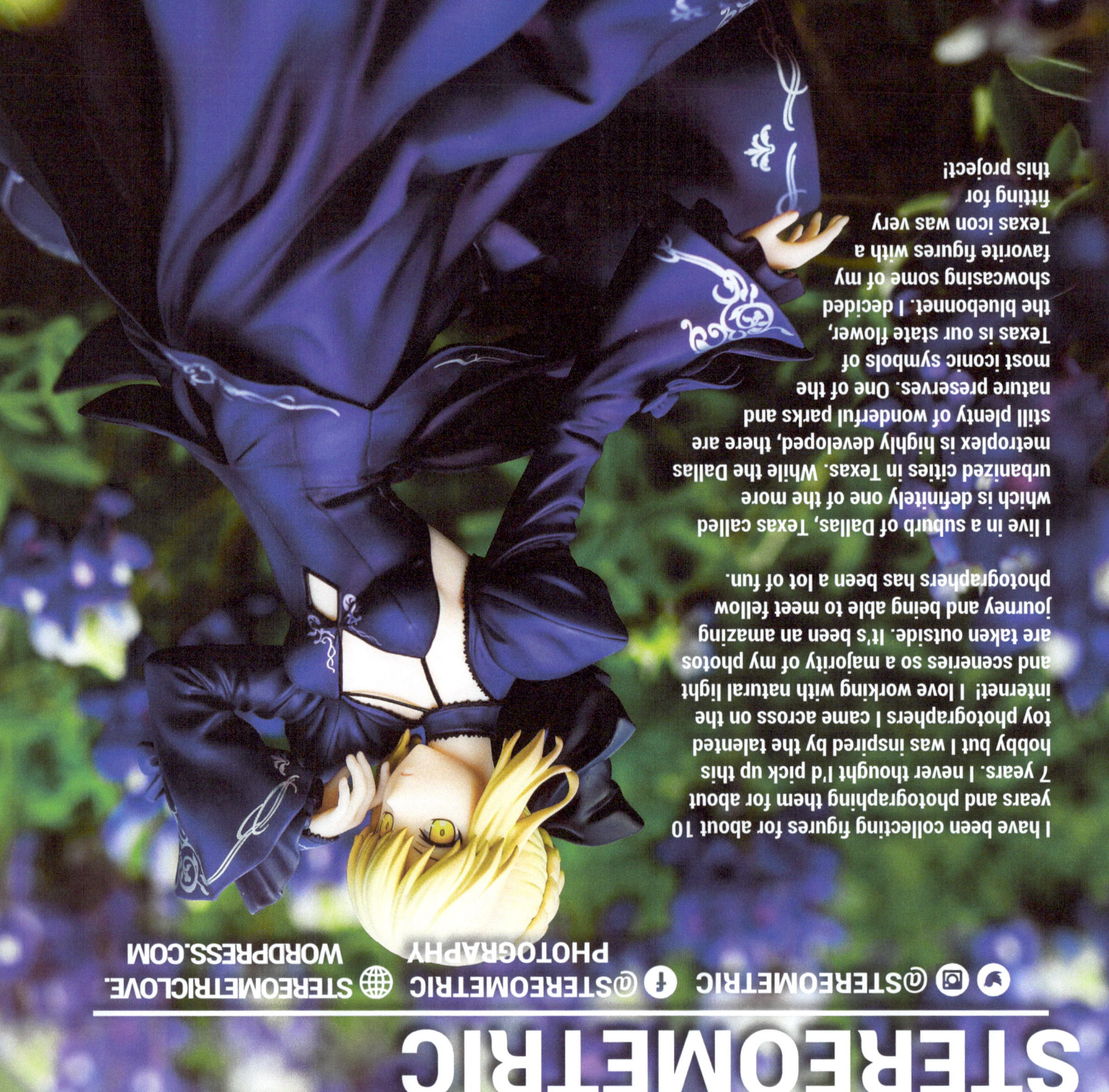

STEREOMETRIC

@STEREOMETRIC PHOTOGRAPHY | @STEREOMETRIC | STEREOMETRICLOVE.WORDPRESS.COM

I have been collecting figures for about 10 years and photographing them for about 7 years. I never thought I'd pick up this hobby but I was inspired by the talented toy photographers I came across on the internet! I love working with natural light and sceneries so a majority of my photos are taken outside. It's been an amazing journey and being able to meet fellow photographers has been a lot of fun.

I live in a suburb of Dallas, Texas called which is definitely one of the more urbanized cities in Texas. While the Dallas metroplex is highly developed, there are still plenty of wonderful parks and nature preserves. One of the most iconic symbols of Texas is our state flower, the bluebonnet. I decided showcasing some of my favorite figures with a Texas icon was very fitting for this project!

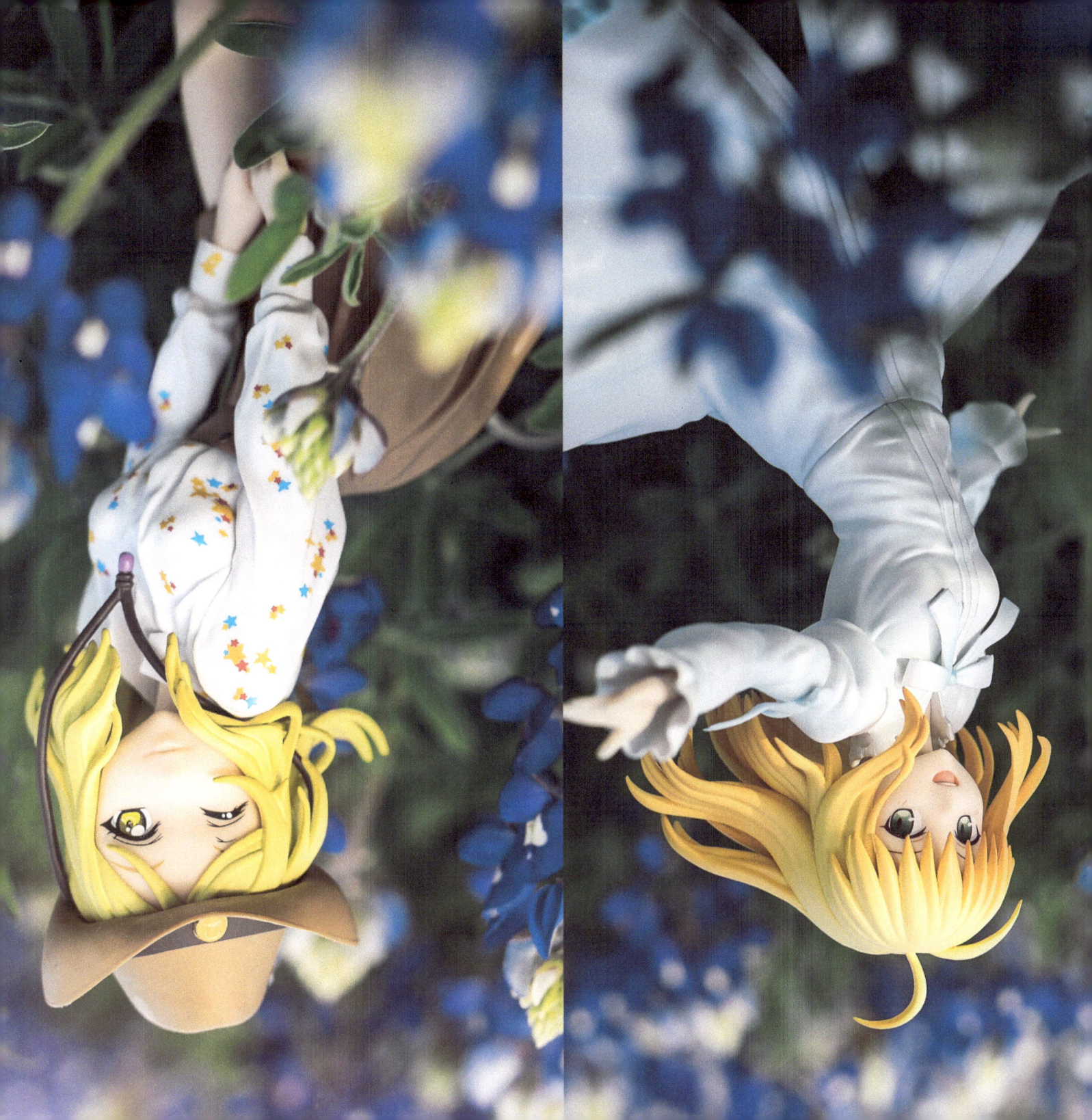

SPECIAL THANKS

PHOTOGRAPHERS

- Kenneth Bolido (fullOanime)
- The Bearded Baka
- 85cmpersecond
- Balance
- The Traveling See
- Isabel (icattails)
- Meta`
- Captain Dangerous
- Miette-chan
- Penguin Otaku Photography
- Stereometric

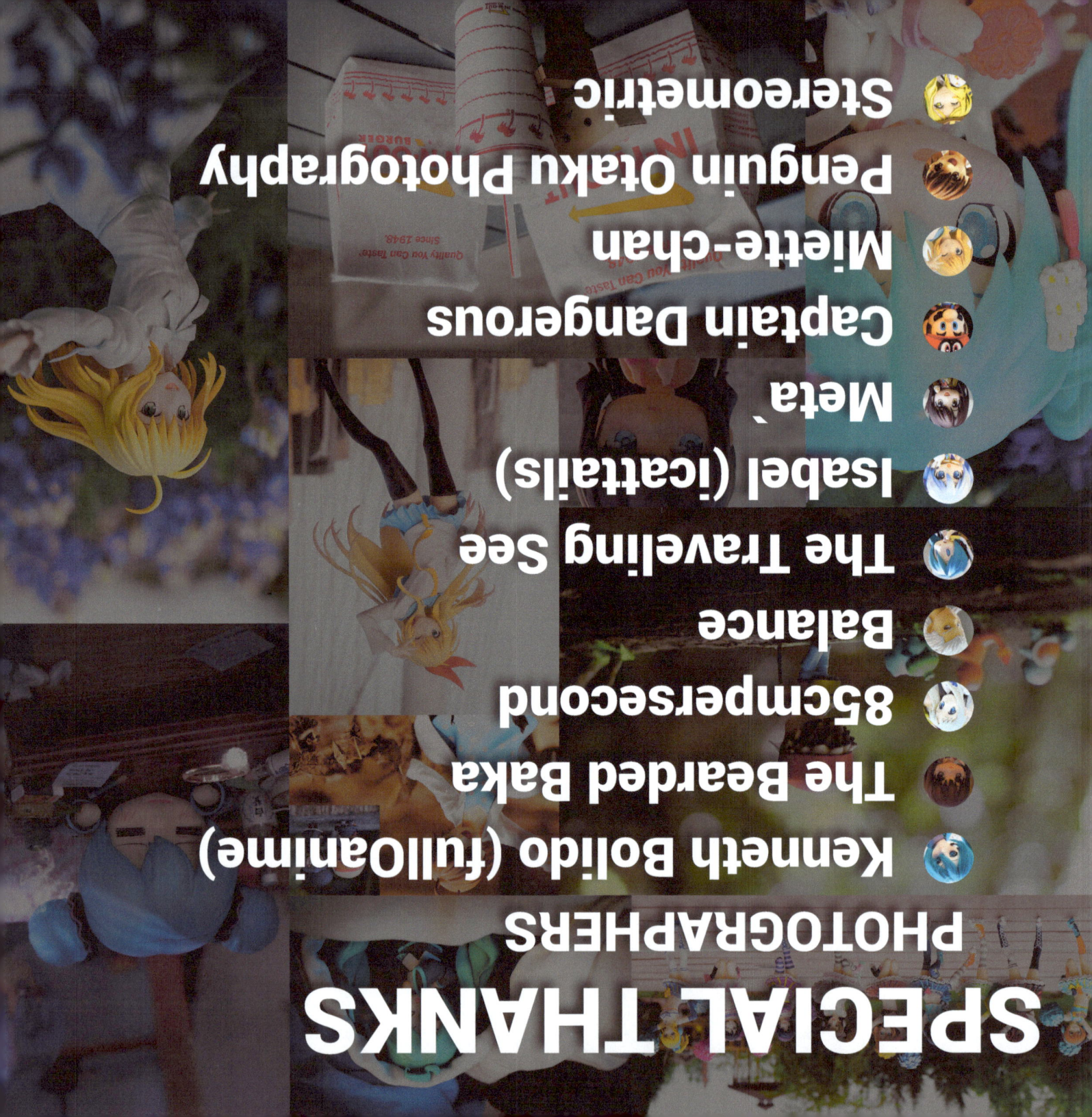

www.ingramcontent.com/pod-product-compliance
Lightning Source LLC
Chambersburg PA
CBHW051821210526
45473CB00005B/1689